SWEET KNITS FOR BABY

30 MODERN AND FRESH DESIGNS FOR 0 - 3 YEARS

JODY LONG

TuVa

Tuva Publishing
www.tuvapublishing.com

Address Merkez Mah. Cavusbasi Cad. No:71
Cekmekoy - Istanbul 34782 / Turkey
Tel: +9 0216 642 62 62

Sweet Knits For Baby

First Print 2019 / October

All Global Copyrights Belong To
Tuva Tekstil ve Yayıncılık Ltd.

Content Knitting

Editor in Chief Ayhan DEMİRPEHLİVAN
Project Editor Kader DEMİRPEHLİVAN
Designer Jody LONG
Technical Editors Leyla ARAS, Büşra ESER
Graphic Designers Ömer ALP, Abdullah BAYRAKÇI, Zilal ÖNEL
Photograph Tuva Publishing

ISBN 978-605-9192-33-0

 TuvaYayincilik TuvaPublishing
 TuvaYayincilik TuvaPublishing

This book is dedicated to my dearest friend Mary Beth Bell who has shown the utmost interest in my design career over the past year and listened to my ideas no matter what time of the day.

This book would not have been possible without the help of the following knitters: Debbie Ince, Kate Gray and Mandy Liddell for working to very tight deadlines under pressure.

Lera for organising the models and styling.

Last but not least the amazing team at Tuva Publishing for producing yet another great book.

Introduction

There is always a great joy amongst family and friends hearing someone is expecting a baby!

In this book you will find the perfect garments and accessories to knit any newborn up to 3 years.

With the trends of today, baby showers are becoming all the rage and there is nothing more satisfying than receiving a hand made garment, knowing that each stitch was made with love and care.

Projects within this book range from easy to more challenging, making this the perfect baby book for all knitters.

The main enjoyment in designing this book was making sure there was a wide variety for boys and girls alike.

Happy Knitting!

Jody Long

contents

BABY KNITS	

p.86

p.90

p.94

p.80

p.96

p.100

p.102

p.106

p.110

p.114

p.122

p.128

p.134

p.118

INFORMATION

ABBREVIATIONS

alt	alternate
beg	begin(ning)
cm	centimetres
cont	continue
dec	decreas(e)(ing)
foll	following
folls	follows
g st	garter stitch (K every row)
inc	increas(e)(ing)
in(s)	inch(es)
K	knit
mm	millimetres
M1	make one stitch by picking up horizontal loop lying before next stitch and knitting into back of it
M1P	make one stitch by picking up horizontal loop lying before next stitch and purling into back of it
meas	measures
P	purl
patt	pattern
psso	pass slipped stitch over
p2sso	pass 2 slipped stitches over
rem	remain(ing)
rep	repeat
rev st st	reverse stocking stitch (1 row P, 1 row K)
RS	right side
sl 1	slip one stitch
sl2togK	slip 2 stitches together knitways as though to K2tog
st(s)	stitch(es)
st st	stocking stitch (1 row K, 1 row P)
tbl	through back of loop
tog	together
WS	wrong side
yo	yarn over
0	no stitches, times or rows
-	no stitches, times or rows for that siz

GLOSSARY

UK	USA
cast off	bind off
stocking stitch	stockinette stitch
moss stitch	seed stitch
double moss stitch	double seed st
tension	gauge

EXPERIENCE RATING

(For guidance only)

For the Beginner Knitter
For the beginner knitter, basic garment shaping and straight forward knitting techniques.

For the Experienced Knitter
Simple straight forward knitting, introducing various, shaping techniques.

For the Advanced Knitter
Advanced techniques used, using advanced stitch patters and garment shaping and more challenging techniques.

ABOUT THE YARN

Jody Long Ciao is 100% extra fine merino wool, which is extra soft with a luxurious feel. Ciao gives great stitch definition whether it be simple textures to complex cables this is a good all round yarn. Merino wool creates 'breathable' knitted fabrics which are cool to wear in warm weather and warm in colder temperatures. Ciao knits to a DK weight. The signature colour palette makes this yarn perfect for the whole family and ideal for babies as it is easy care.

CARING FOR THE YARN

Jody Long Ciao is machine washable at 30°c, cool iron and dry flat away from direct sunlight.

Do not tumble dry, bleach or wring out excess water, but press lightly between two clean cotton towels to remove excess moisture.

INFORMATION

TENSION

Obtaining the correct tension is perhaps the single factor which can make the difference between a successful garment and a disastrous one. It controls both the shape and size of a garment, so any variation, however slight, can distort the finished garment. We recommend that you knit a square in pattern and/or stocking stitch (depending on the pattern instructions) of 5 - 10 more stitches and 5 - 10 more rows than those given in the tension note. Mark out the
central 10 cm (4 in) square with pins. If you have too many stitches to 10 cm (4 in) try again using thicker needles, if you have too few stitches to 10 cm (4 in) try again using finer needles. Once you have matched the correct tension you garment will be knitted to the measurements indicated in the size diagram (schematic) shown at the end of each pattern.

WORKING FROM A CHART

Many of the patterns in this bookl are worked from charts. Each square on a chart represents a stitch and each line of squares a row of knitting. Each colour used is given a different letter and these are shown in the material section, or in the key alongside the chart of each pattern. When working from the charts, read odd rows (K) from right to left and even rows (P) from left to right, unless otherwise stated. When working lace from a chart it is vitally important to note that all but largest size may have to alter the first and last few stitches in order not to lose or gain stitches over rows (see woking a lace pattern.)

WORKING IN A LACE PATTERN

When working in a lace pattern it is very important to remember that if you are unable to work both the increase and corresponding decrease and visa versa, then the stitches should be worked in stocking stitch.

FINISHING GARMENTS

After working for hours knitting a garment, it seems a great pity that many garments are spoiled because such little care is taken in the pressing and finishing process. Follow the text below for a professional finished garment.

Block out each piece of knitting and following the instructions on the ball band press the garment pieces, omitting the ribs, Tip: Take special care to press the edges, as this will make sewing up both easier and neater. If the ball indicates that the fabric is not to be pressed, then covering the blocked out fabric with a damp white cotton cloth and leaving it flat to dry naturally out of direct sunlight will have the desired effect. Darn in all loose ends neatly along the selvage edge or a colour join, as appropriate.

SEAMING THE GARMENTS

When seaming the pieces together, remember to match areas of colour and/or texture very carefully where they meet. Use a blunt wool needle to prevent splitting the yarn/stitches while seaming. Use a seam stitch such as backstitch or mattress stitch for all main knitting seams and join all ribs and neckband with mattress stitch, unless otherwise stated.

KNITTING WITH COLOUR

There are two main methods of working with colour in knitting: Intarsia and Fair isle techniques. The first method produces a single thickness of fabric and is usually used where a colour is only required in a particular area of a row and does not form a repeating pattern across the row, as in the fair isle technique.

Fair isle type knitting: When two or three colours are worked repeatedly across a row, strand the yarn not in use loosely behind the stitches being worked. If you are working with more than two colours, treat the "floating" yarns as if they were one yarn and always spread the stitches to their correct width to keep them elastic. It is advisable not to carry the stranded or "floating" yarns over more than three stitches at a time, but to weave them under and over the colour you are working. The "floating" yarns are therefore caught neatly at the back of the work.

Intarsia type knitting: The simplest way to do this is cut short lengths of yarn for each motif or block of colour used in a row. Then joining in the various colours at the appropriate point on the row, link one colour to the next by twisting them around each other where they meet on wrong side to avoid holes forming. All ends can then either be weaved along the colour lines, as each motif is completed or they can be "knitted-in" to the fabric of the knitting as each colour is worked into the pattern. This is done in much the same way as "weaving-in" yarns when working the Fair isle technique and does save time darning-in ends. It is essential that the tension is noted for intarsia as this may vary from stocking stitch if both are used in the same pattern.

Techniques

Not every knitter holds their needles and yarn in the same way. The yarn can be held in either the right or left hand, the needles can be held from above or below. Try each of the methods described here and work in a way that is most comfortable for you. They are all bound to feel awkward and slow at first.

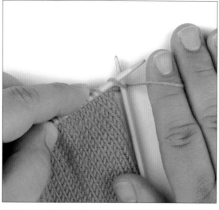

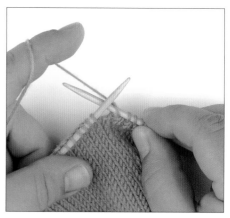

**English method
(yarn in the right hand)**

Left hand: hold the needle with the stitches in your left hand with your thumb lying along the needle, your index finger resting on top near the tip and the remaining fingers curled under the needle to support it. The thumb and the index finger control the stitches and the tip of the needle.

Right hand: pass the yarn over the index finger, under the middle and over the third finger. The yarn lies between the nail and the first joint and the index finger 'throws' the yarn around the right-hand needle when knitting. The yarn should be able to move freely and is tensioned between the middle and third finger. You can wrap the yarn around the little finger if you feel it is too loose and it keeps falling off your fingers. Hold the empty needle in your right hand with your thumb lying along the needle, your index finger near the tip and the remaining fingers curled under the needle to support it (see right hand in Continental method).

Some knitters prefer to hold the end of the right-hand needle under their right arm, anchoring it firmly. Whilst knitting this needle remains still and the right hand is above the needle and moves the yarn around it.

Alternative grip

Left hand: hold the needle in the same way as shown above left.

Right hand: hold the yarn in the fingers the same way as shown above. Hold the needle like a pen, on top of the hand between thumb and index finger. The end of the needle will be above your right arm, in the crook of the elbow. As the fabric grows longer, the thumb will hold the needle behind the knitting.

**Continental method
(yarn in the left hand)**

Left hand: wrap the yarn around your little finger, under the middle two fingers and then over the index finger between the nail and the first joint. The yarn is held taut between the index finger and the needle. Hold the needle with your thumb lying along the needle, your index finger near the tip and remaining fingers curled under the needle to support it. The thumb and index finger control the stitches, yarn and needle tip.

Right hand: hold the empty needle in your right hand with your thumb lying along the needle, index finger resting on top near the tip and remaining fingers curled under the needle to support it. The thumb and index finger control the stitches and the needle tip, which hooks the yarn and draws the loop through.

To begin knitting, you need to work a foundation row of stitches called casting on. There are several ways to cast on depending on the type of edge that you want. The cast on edge should be firm; too loose and it will look untidy and flare out, too tight and it will break and the stitches unravel. If your casting on is always too tight, use a size larger needle. If it is always too loose, use a size smaller needle. Remember to change back to the correct size needle to begin knitting.

Thumb method
This is the simplest way of casting on and you will need only one needle.

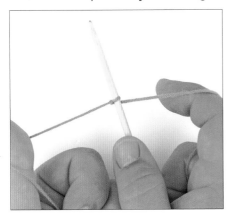 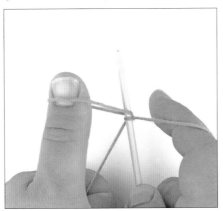 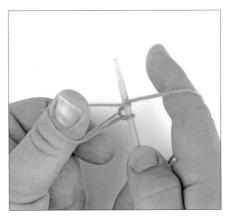

1. Make a slip knot some distance from the end of the yarn (see Knit Perfect) and place it on the needle. Hold the needle in your right hand. Pass the ball end of the yarn over the index finger, under the middle and then over the third finger. Holding the free end of yarn in your left hand, wrap it around your left thumb from front to back.

2. Insert the needle through the thumb loop from front to back.

3. Wrap the ball end over the needle.

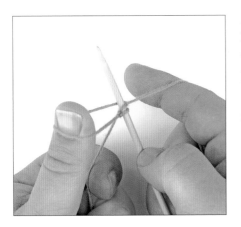

4. Pull a new loop through the thumb loop by passing the thumb loop over the end of the needle. Remove your thumb and tighten the new loop on the needle by pulling the free end. Continue in this way until you have cast on the required number of stitches.

The slip knot counts as the first cast on stitch. It is made some distance from the end of the yarn and placed on the needle. Pull the ends of the yarn to tighten it. You now have two ends of yarn coming from the slip knot; the ball end attached to the ball and a shorter free end.

For the thumb method of casting on, you will need approximately 1in (2.5cm) for every stitch you want to cast on. When you have cast on, you should have at least a 6in (15cm) length to sew in.

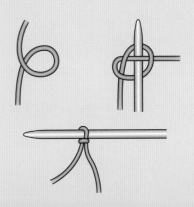

In knitting there are only two stitches to learn - knit stitch (K) and purl stitch (P). They are the foundation of all knitted fabrics. Once you have mastered these two simple stitches, by combining them in different ways you will soon be knitting ribs, textures, cables and many more exciting fabrics.

English Method (yarn in the right hand)
In knit stitch the yarn is held at the back of the work (the side facing away from you) and is made up of four steps.

1. Hold the needle with the cast on stitches in your left hand, and insert the right-hand needle into the front of the stitch from left to right.

2. Pass the yarn under and around the right-hand needle.

3. Pull the new loop on the right-hand needle through the stitch on the left-hand needle.

4. Slip the stitch off the left-hand needle. One knit stitch is completed.

To continue...
Repeat these four steps for each stitch on the left-hand needle. All the stitches on the left-hand needle will be transferred to the right -hand needle where the new row is formed. At the end of the row, swap the needle with the stitches into your left hand and the empty needle into your right hand, and work the next row in the same way.

BINDING (CASTING) OFF

1. Knit two stitches, insert the tip of left-hand needle into the front of the first stitch on the right-hand needle. Lift this stitch over the second stitch and off the needle.

2. One stitch is left on the right-hand needle. Knit the next stitch and lift the second stitch over this and off the needle. Continue in this way until one stitch remains on the right-hand needle.

3. To finish, cut the yarn (leaving a length long enough to sew in), thread the end through the last stitch and slip it off the needle. Pull the yarn end to tighten the stitch and secure.

Bind (cast) off purlwise
To bind (cast) off on a purl row, simply purl the stitches instead of knitting them.

You may find purl stitch a little harder to learn than knit stitch. But really it is just the reverse of a knit stitch. If you purled every row, you would produce garter stitch (the same as if you knitted every row). It is not often that you will work every row in purl stitch; it is easier and faster to knit every row if you want garter stitch.

English method (yarn in the right hand)
In purl stitch the yarn is held at the front of the work (the side facing you) and is made up of four steps.

1. Hold the needle with the cast on stitches in your left hand, and insert the right-hand needle into the front of the stitch from right to left.

2. Pass the yarn over and around the right-hand needle.

3. Pull the new loop on the right-hand needle through the stitch on the left-hand needle.

4. Slip the stitch off the left-hand needle. One stitch is completed.

To continue...
Repeat these four steps for each stitch on the left-hand needle. All the stitches on the left-hand needle will be transferred to the right-hand needle where the new purl row is formed. At the end of the row, swap the needle with the stitches into your left hand and the empty needle into your right hand, and work the next row in the same way.

To shape knitting, stitches are increased or decreased. Increases are used to make a piece of knitting wider by adding more stitches, either on the ends of rows or within the knitting.

Some increases are worked to be invisible whilst others are meant to be seen and are known as decorative increases. You can increase one stitch at a time or two or more.

Increasing one stitch

The easiest way to increase one stitch is to work into the front and back of the same stitch. This produces a small bar across the second (increase) satitch and is very visible. This makes counting the increases easier.

On a knit row (Kfb)

1. Knit into the front of the stitch as usual, do not slip the stitch off the left-hand needle but knit into it again through the back of the loop.

2. Slip the original stitch off the left-hand needle. You have now increased an extra stitch and you can see the bar (increased stitch) to the left of the original stitch.

> **To make a neater edge** when working increases at the beginning and end of rows, work the increase stitches a few stitches from the end. This leaves a continuous stitch up the edge of the fabric that makes sewing up easier. Because the made stitch lies to the left of the original stitch, at the beginning of a knit row you knit one stitch, then make the increase, but at the end of a knit row you work the increase into the third stitch from the end. The increase stitch lies between the second and third stitches at each end.
>
> On a purl row you work in exactly the same way; the bar will be in the correct position two stitches from either end.

On a purl row (Pfb)

3. Purl into the front of the stitch as usual, do not slip the stitch off the left-hand needle but purl into it again through the back of the loop.

4. Slip the original stitch off the left-hand needle. You have now increased an extra stitch and you can see the bar (increased stitch) to the left of the original stitch.

This is another way to increase one stitch and is often used where increasing stitches after a rib. The new stitch is made between two existing stitches using the horizontal thread that lies between the stitches - called the running thread. This is an invisible increase and is harder to see when counting.

On a knit row (M1)

1. Knit to the point where the increase is to be made. Insert the tip of the left-hand needle under the running thread from front to back.

2. Knit this loop through the back to twist it. By twisting the stitch it will prevent leaving a hole appearing where the made stitch is.

On a purl row (M1P)

To work this increase on a purl row, work as given for the knit way but instead purl into the back of the loop.

Increasing more than one stitch

To increase two stitches simply knit into the front, back and then the front again of the same stitch. When knitting bobbles, you will sometimes make five, six or seven stitches out of one stitch in this way. For example, to make seven stitches the instructions would read (k into front and back of same st) 3 times, then k into front again.

MATTRESS STITCH

This technique produces a discreet seam that is especially good if the edge stitches are not very neat, as they become part of the seam inside the project. The other advantage of mattress stitch is that it is worked from the right side of work, so the neatness of the seam can be assessed as the seam is stitched and adjustments made immediately, rather than having to painstakingly unpick the whole seam. Careful preparation will pay dividends, so press and block the pieces first if required, paying particular attention to the edge stitches. Then pin the seams together and matching pattern if there is any to be matched.

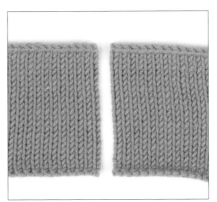

1. Place the edges that need seaming together with right sides of work facing you.

3. The neatest seam is achieved by pulling the yarn just enough to pull the stitches together.

2. Working from the bottom, and between the first and second stitch in from the edge, pass the needle under the loops of two rows on one side; then pass the needle under the loops of the corresponding two rows on other side. Work a few stitches like this before drawing the first stitches tight as this will help to keep track of the line of the seam.

Decreasing is used at the ends of rows or within the knitted fabric to reduce the number of stitches being worked on. This means that you can shape your knitted fabric by making it narrower.

Decreasing one stitch

The simplest way to decrease one stitch is to knit or purl two stitches together (K2tog or P2tog). Both of these methods produce the same result on the front (knit side) of the work; the decrease slopes to the right.

(K2tog or P2tog). Both of these methods produce the same result on the front (knit side) of the work; the decrease slopes to the right.

P2tog on a p row Purl to where the decrease is to be, insert the right-hand needle (as though to purl) through the next two stitches and purl them together as one stitch.

> Always read how to work a decrease very carefully. Some of them have similar abbreviations with only a slight difference between them.
> In patterns the designer may use different abbreviations to those given here. Always check the detailed explanation of abbreviations.

K2tog tbl on a k row Knit to where the decrease is to be, insert the right-hand needle through the back of the next two stitches and knit them together as one stitch.

P2tog tbl on a p row Purl to where the decrease is to be, insert the right-hand needle through the back of the next two stitches and purl them together as one stitch.

Decorative decreasing one stitch purlwise

Sometimes decreases are decorative, especially in lace knitting where they form part of the pattern. Then you have to be aware of whether the decrease slants right or left. Each decrease has an opposite and the two of them are called a pair. There is one way to work the decrease that is the pair to p2tog which slopes to the left when seen on the front (knit side) of the work.

There are two ways to work the decrease that is the pair to K2tog. They both produce the same result and slope to the left.

Slip one, slip one, knit two together (SSK)

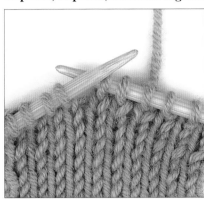

1. Slip two stitches knitwise one at a time from left-hand needle to right-hand needle.

2. Insert the left-hand needle from left to right through the fronts of these two stitches and knit together as one stitch.

Slip one, knit one, pass slipped stitch over (SKPO)

1. Insert the right-hand needle knitwise into the next stitch.

2. Slip it on to the right-hand needle without knitting it, then knit the next stitch.

3. With the tip of the left-hand needle, lift the slipped stitch over the knitted stitch and off the needle. This is like binding (casting) off one stitch.

Slip two, knit one, pass the two slipped stitches over (SK2PO)

1. Insert the right-hand needle knitwise into the next two stitches as if to knit two stitches together without knitting them, slip the two stitches from left-hand needle to right-hand needle.

2. Knit the next stitch, then with the tip of left-hand needle, lift the two slipped stitches over the knitted stitch and off the needle.

3. You have now completed the central double decrease.

Knit every row

When you knit every row the fabric you make is called garter stitch (g st) and has rows of raised ridges on the front and back of the fabric. It looks the same on the back and the front so it is reversible. Garter stitch lies flat, is quite a thick fabric and does not curl at the edges. These qualities make it ideal for borders and collars, as well as for scarves and the main fabric of a garment.

CABLES

Cable knitting always looks more difficult then it actual is. It is simply done by using a cable needle (third needle) to temporarily hold stitches to be transferred to the front or back of your work. Always remember if the cable needle is at the back of work then the cable will lean to the right. If the cable needle is at the front of work then the cable will lean to the left. There are many different cables, always read the instructions and abbreviations carefully as they may look alike or other designers may use different abbreviations. The number of stitches to be moved will be stated in the pattern. Normally cables are worked only on the right side of work, however I have been known to design garments with cables on the wrong side of work too.

Cable front

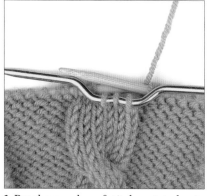

1. Put the number of stitches stated onto a cable needle.

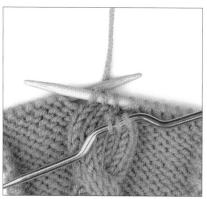

2. Position the cable needle at the front of the work and knit or purl the stated number of stitches from the left-hand needle.

3. Then knit or purl the stated number of stitches from the cable needle.

Cable back

Cable back differs only in that the stitches slipped onto the cable needle are held at the back of the work while the stitches are knitted or purled from the left-hand needle.

Seed (Moss) stitch
Alternate one knit stitch with one purl stitch to the end of the row. On the next row, knit all the purl stitches and purl and the knit stitches as they face you.

1x1 RIB
Alternate one knit stitch with one purl stitch to the end of the row. On the next row, knit all the knit stitches and purl all the purl stitches as they face you.

Simple lace is made up of yarn overs to make a stitch with a pairing decrease to keep the stitch count the same on each row. More complicated lace may have variable stitch counts.

No matter which one you are working the rules are the same; If you do not have enough stitches to decrease a yarn over then work this stitch plain and vice versa.

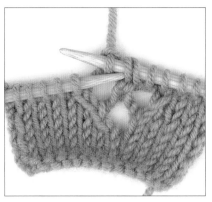

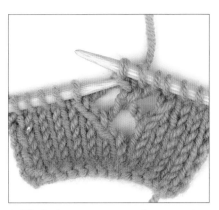

1. Knit to where the pattern states and work a yarn over, by taking the yarn under and over the needle to create a stitch.

2. Work the next two stitches together and work to the end of the row.

3. After working several rows of lace pattern it becomes easier to follow your knitting.

INTARSIA

Intarsia is a technique of color knitting used when the color forms blocks within a design. The word intarsia describes the method of securing the blocks of color together.

It forms a single layer fabric, which means it is economical with yarn and has a drop similar to a single color fabric. (see page 11) on how to read a chart.

1. Using the color stated in the pattern knit to where the color needs to be changed. Then insert the right-hand needle into the next stitch, and pass the new color under the last color before working the next stitch.

2. The technique is exactly the same for a purl row. The reason you must twisting the yarn colors together as they meet is to avoid leaving a hole.

3. When working a straight color change you will notice you have colored vertical lines on the wrong side of your knitting if you are working the intarsia method correctly. If you work a diagonal color change the colored line where the yarns meet will also run diagonally.

PROJECTS

SKILL LEVEL

ALBERTO

SIZE

AGE	0-6 months	6-12 months	1-2 years	2-3 years
To fit chest				
	41	46	51	56 cm
	16	18	20	22 in
Actual chest measurement				
	45	51	56	62 cm
	17¾	20	22	24¼ in
Full length, from back neck				
	24	28	32	38 cm
	9½	11	12½	15 in
Sleeve length				
	15	17	20	24 cm
	6	6½	8	9½ in

YARN

Jody Long Ciao
3 [4: 5: 5] x 50g balls in Cornflower 009

NEEDLES

1 pair 3.25 mm (no 10) (US 3) needles
1 pair 4 mm (no 8) (US 6) needles
Cable needle

BUTTONS - 3 [3: 0: 0]

TENSION

22 sts and 30 rows to 10 cm (4 in) measured over st st, 26 sts and 34 rows to 10 cm (4 in) measured over textured patt, both using 4 mm (US 6) needles.

ABBREVIATIONS

See inside front flap

SPECIAL ABBREVIATIONS

C4B = slip next 2 sts onto a cable needle and leave at back of work, K2, then K2 from cable needle.
C4F = slip next 2 sts onto a cable needle and leave at front of work, K2, then K2 from cable needle.

BACK

Using 3.25 mm (US 3) needles cast on 52 [60: 64: 70] sts.
Beg with a K row, work 3 [3: 5: 5] rows in st st, ending with **WS** facing for next row.
Inc row (WS): P6 [5: 7: 7], M1P, (P8 [10: 10: 8], M1P), 5 [5: 5: 7] times, P6 [5: 7: 7]. 58 [66: 70: 78] sts. Place a marker at each end of last row.
Now work in rib as folls:
Row 1 (RS): *K2, P2, rep from * to last 2 sts, K2.
Row 2: *P2, K2, rep from * to last 2 sts, P2.
These 2 rows form rib.
Cont in rib for a further 7 [7: 9: 9] rows, ending with **WS** facing for next row.
Dec row (WS): P4 [5: 6: 2], P2tog, (P5 [4: 6: 6], P2tog), 7 [9: 7: 9] times, P3 [5: 6: 2]. 50 [56: 62: 68] sts.
Change to 4 mm (US 6) needles.
Beg with a K row, work in st st until Back meas 12 [14: 16: 20] cm (4¾ [5½: 6¼: 8] in), from markers and ending with **WS** facing for next row.
Now work in ridge patt as folls:
Row 1 (WS): Knit.
Rows 2 and 3: Purl.
Rows 4 and 5: Knit.
Rows 6 and 7: As rows 2 and 3.
Inc row (RS): K4 [7: 2: 5] (inc knitwise into next st) twice, *K6, (inc knitwise into next st) twice, rep from * to last 4 [7: 2: 5] sts, K4 [7: 2: 5]. 62 [68: 78: 84] sts.
Now work in textured patt from chart as folls:
Beg and ending rows as indicated, foll appropriate chart for size being knitted, repeating the 4 row patt repeat throughout and noting that chart row 1 is a **WS** row, cont in patt from chart as folls:

Cont in textured patt until Back meas 24 [28: 32: 38] cm (9½ [11: 12½: 15] in), ending with RS facing for next row.

Shape Shoulders

Keeping patt correct, cast off 9 [10: 12: 13] sts at beg of next 2 rows, then 10 [11: 13: 14] sts at beg of foll 2 rows.
(**Note:** To stop shoulder seam stretching too much, dec 2 sts at top of each cable. Number of sts stated relates to original number of sts and does NOT take into account any decreased st.)
Break yarn and leave rem 24 [26: 28: 30] sts on a holder (for Neckband).

FRONT

Work as given for Back until 16 [18: 20: 20] rows less have been worked than on Back to beg of shoulder shaping, ending with RS facing for next row.

Shape Front Neck

Next row (RS): Patt 26 [29: 34: 36] and turn, leaving rem sts on a holder.
Dec 1 st at neck edge of next 2 rows, then on foll 5 [6: 7: 7] alt rows. 19 [21: 25: 27] sts.
Work 1 [1: 3: 3] rows, ending with RS facing for next row.
(**Note:** For 1st and 2nd sizes, this shoulder edge is 2 rows lower than right shoulder as the buttonhole border will be added.)

Shape Shoulder

Keeping patt correct, cast off 9 [10: 12: 13] sts at beg of next row.
Work 1 row.
Cast off rem 10 [11: 13: 14] sts.
Return to sts on holder and slip central 10 [10: 10: 12] sts onto another holder (for Neckband). Rejoin yarn to rem sts and patt to end. 26 [29: 34: 36] sts.
Dec 1 st at neck edge of next 2 rows, then on foll 5 [6: 7: 7] alt rows. 19 [21: 25: 27] sts.
Work 4 rows, ending with **WS** facing for next row.

Shape Shoulder

Keeping patt correct, cast off 9 [10: 12: 13] sts at beg of next row.
Work 1 row.
Cast off rem 10 [11: 13: 14] sts.

SLEEVES

Using 3.25 mm (US 3) needles cast on 38 [38: 42: 42] sts.
Beg with a K row, work 3 [3: 5: 5] rows in st st, ending with **WS** facing for next row.
Inc row (WS): P7 [7: 6: 6], M1P, (P8 [8: 10: 10], M1P), 3 times, P7 [7: 6: 6]. 42 [42: 46: 46] sts. Place a marker at each end of last row.
Work in rib as given for Back for 9 [9: 11: 11] rows, ending with **WS** facing for next row.
Dec row (WS): P3 [3: 1: 2], P2tog, (P5 [5: 4: 6], P2tog) 5 [5: 7: 5] times, P2 [2: 1: 2]. 36 [36: 38: 40] sts.
Change to 4 mm (US 6) needles.
Beg with a K row, work in st st as folls:
Inc 1 st at each end of 3rd [next: next: next] and every foll 6th [6th: 8th: 8th] row to 40 [42: 44: 48] sts.
Work 2 [0: 0: 0] rows straight, ending with **WS** facing for next row.

Now work in ridge patt and still shaping sleeve seam as folls:
Row 1 (WS): Knit.
Rows 2 and 3: Purl.
Row 4: (Inc knitwise into first st) 1 [0: 0: 0] times, K to last 1 [0: 0: 0] st, (inc knitwise into last st) 1 [0: 0: 0] times. 42 [42: 44: 48] sts.
Row 5: Knit.
Row 6: (Inc **purlwise** into first st) 0 [1: 1: 0] times, P to last 0 [1: 1: 0] st, (inc **purlwise** into last st) 0 [1: 1: 0] times. 42 [44: 46: 48] sts.
Row 7: Purl.
Inc row (RS): K8 [9: 10: 3] (inc knitwise into next st) twice, *K6, (inc knitwise into next st) twice, rep from * to last 8 [9: 10: 3] sts, K8 [9: 10: 3]. 50 [52: 54: 60] sts.
Now work in textured patt from sleeve chart as folls:
Beg and ending rows as indicated, foll appropriate chart for size being knitted, repeating the 4 row patt repeat throughout and noting that chart row 1 is a **WS** row **and at same time** inc 1 st at each end of 8th [6th: 6th: 2nd] and then on - [1: 2: 2] foll - [6th: 8th: 10th] rows, taking inc sts into patt. 52 [56: 60: 66] sts.
Cont in textured patt until Sleeve meas 15 [17: 20: 24] cm (6 [6½: 8: 9½] in), from markers and ending with RS facing for next row.

Shape Top

Keeping patt correct, cast off 6 [6: 7: 7] sts at beg of next 4 rows, then 6 [7: 6: 8] sts at beg of foll 2 rows.
Cast off rem 16 [18: 20: 22] sts.

MAKING UP

Join right shoulder seam.

Neckband

With RS facing, using 3.25 mm (US 3) needles, pick up and knit 14 [15: 18: 18] sts down left side of front neck, K across 10 [10: 10: 12] sts on front holder, pick up and knit 14 [15: 18: 18] sts up right side of front neck, then K across 24 [26: 28: 30] sts on back holder. 62 [66: 74: 78] sts.
Now work in rib as folls:
Row 1 (WS): *P2, K2, rep from * to last 2 sts, P2.
Row 2: *K2, P2, rep from * to last 2 sts, K2.
These 2 rows form rib.
Cont in rib for a further 3 [3: 5: 5] rows, ending with RS facing for next row. Place a marker at each end of last row.
Dec row (RS): K11 [11: 8: 8], K2tog, (K11 [12: 9: 10], K2tog), 3 [3: 5: 5] times, K12 [11: 9: 8]. 58 [62: 68: 72] sts.
Beg with a P row, work 3 [3: 5: 5] rows in st st, ending with RS facing for next row.
Cast off **very loosely** knitwise.

For 1st and 2nd Sizes Only
Back Button Border

With RS facing, using 3.25 mm (US 3) needles, pick up and knit 21 [23] sts evenly across left back shoulder edge, from marker on neckband to armhole edge.
Work in g st for 4 rows, ending with **WS** facing for next row.
Cast off **knitwise** (on **WS**).

Front Buttonhole Border

With RS facing, using 3.25 mm (US 3) needles, pick up and knit 21 [23] sts evenly across left front shoulder edge, from armhole edge to marker on neckband.

Row 1 (WS): Knit.

Row 2: K4, (yo, K2tog (to make a buttonhole), K5 [6]) twice, yo, K2tog (to make 3rd buttonhole), K1.

Work in g st for a further 2 rows, ending with **WS** facing for next row.

Cast off **knitwise** (on **WS**).

Lay Front Buttonhole Border over Back Button Border so that borders overlap. Sew together at armhole edge. Attach buttons to correspond with buttonholes.

For 3rd and 4th Sizes only

Join left shoulder and neckband seam to marker then reverse seam for last 6 rows of "st st roll".

For All Sizes

Mark points along side seam edges 10 [11: 12: 13] cm (4 [4¼: 4¾: 5] in) either side of shoulder seams, then sew shaped cast-off edge of sleeve to back and front between these points. Join side seams, reversing seam for first 6 [6: 8: 8] rows for "st st roll". Join sleeve seams, reversing first 6 [6: 8: 8] rows for "st st roll".

Pin out garment to measurements given, cover with damp cloths and leave to dry naturally. See ball band for washing and further care instructions.

Front

Back

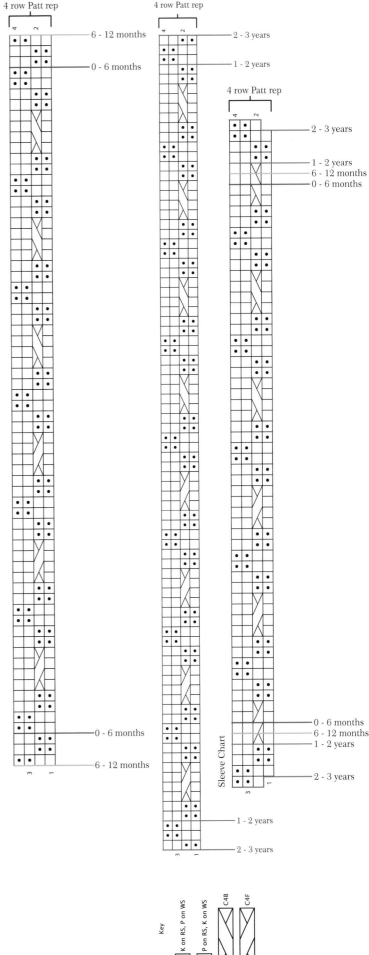

25

SKILL LEVEL

ALESSANDRO

SIZE

AGE	0-6 months	6-12 months	1-2 years	2-3 years
To fit chest				
	41	46	51	56 cm
	16	18	20	22 in
Actual chest measurement				
	46	51	56	61 cm
	18	20	22	24 in
Full length, from shoulder				
	24	28	32	38 cm
	9½	11	12½	15 in
Sleeve length				
	15	17	20	24 cm
	6	6½	8	9½ in

YARN

Jody Long Ciao
A 1 [1: 2: 2] x 50g balls in Lead 003
B 1 [2: 2: 3] x 50g balls in Alabaster 002
C 1 [2: 2: 3] x 50g balls in Cornflower 009

NEEDLES

1 pair 3.25 mm (no 10) (US 3) needles
1 pair 4 mm (no 8) (US 6) needles
3.25 mm (no 10) (US 3) circular needle

BUTTONS - 5 [5: 5: 6]

TENSION

22 sts and 30 rows to 10 cm (4 in) measured over striped st st using 4 mm (US 6) needles.

ABBREVIATIONS

See inside front flap

BACK

Using 3.25 mm (US 3) needles and yarn **A** cast on 58 [66: 70: 74] sts.
Row 1 (RS): K2, *P2, K2, rep from * to end.
Row 2: P2, *K2, P2, rep from * to end.
These 2 rows form rib.
Cont in rib for a further 7 [7: 9: 9] rows, ending with **WS** facing for next row.
Next row (WS): Rib 7 [4: 6: 6], work 2 tog, (rib 5 [5: 5: 8], work 2 tog), 6 [8: 8: 6] times, rib 7 [4: 6: 6]. 51 [57: 61: 67] sts.
Change to 4 mm (US 6) needles.
Beg with a K row, now work in striped st st as folls:
Using yarn **B**, work 2 rows.
Using yarn **C**, work 2 rows.
These 4 rows form striped st st.
Cont in striped st st until Back meas 24 [28: 32: 38] cm (9½ [11: 12½: 15] in), ending with RS facing for next row.

Shape Shoulders

Keeping stripes correct, cast off 9 [9: 10: 11] sts at beg of next 2 rows, then 8 [9: 9: 10] sts at beg of foll 2 rows. 17 [21: 23: 25] sts.
Break yarn and leave sts on a holder (for Neckband).

POCKET LININGS (Make 2)

Using 4 mm (US 6) needles and yarn **A** cast on 12 [13: 14: 15] sts.

Beg with a K row, work in st st for 12 [14: 16: 20] rows, ending with RS facing for next row.

Break yarn and leave sts on a holder.

LEFT FRONT

Using 3.25 mm (US 3) needles and yarn **A** cast on 27 [31: 31: 35] sts.

Row 1 (RS): K2, *P2, K2, rep from * to last st, K1.

Row 2: K1, *P2, K2, rep from * to last 2 sts, P2.

These 2 rows form rib.

Cont in rib for a further 7 [7: 9: 9] rows, ending with **WS** facing for next row.

Next row (WS): Rib 4 [3: 5: 5], work 2 tog, (rib 4 [4: 8: 6], work 2 tog) 3 [4: 2: 3] times, rib 3 [2: 4: 4]. 23 [26: 28: 31] sts.

Change to 4 mm (US 6) needles.

Beg with a K row, work in striped st st as given for Back as folls:

Work 15 [19: 23: 27] rows, ending with stripe row 3 and **WS** facing for next row.

Place Pocket

Keeping stripes correct throughout, work as folls:

Next row (WS): P8 [9: 9: 10], cast off next 12 [13: 14: 15] sts **knitwise** (for pocket opening), P to end.

Next row (RS): K3 [4: 5: 6], with RS facing K across 12 [13: 14:15] sts of first Pocket Lining, K to end. 23 [26: 28: 31] sts.

Cont in striped st st until Left Front meas 22 [30: 34: 38] rows less than Back to start of shoulder shaping, ending with RS facing for next row.

Shape Front Neck Slope

Keeping stripes correct, work as folls:

Next row (RS): K to last 4 sts, K2tog, K2. 22 [25: 27: 30] sts.

Working all neck decreases as set by last row, dec 1 st at neck edge of 2nd and every foll 4th row until 17 [18: 19: 21] sts rem.

Work 3 rows, ending with RS facing for next row.

Shape Shoulder

Keeping stripes correct, cast off 9 [9: 10: 11] sts at beg of next row.

Work 1 row.

Cast off rem 8 [9: 9: 10] sts.

RIGHT FRONT

Using 3.25 mm (US 3) needles and yarn **A** cast on 27 [31: 31: 35] sts.

Row 1 (RS): K1, *K2, P2, rep from * to last 2 sts, K2.

Row 2: *P2, K2, rep from * to last 3 sts, P2, K1.

These 2 rows form rib.

Cont in rib for a further 7 [7: 9: 9] rows, ending with **WS** facing for next row.

Next row (WS): Rib 3 [2: 4: 4], work 2 tog, (rib 4 [4: 8: 6], work 2 tog) 3 [4: 2: 3] times, rib 4 [3: 5: 5]. 23 [26: 28: 31] sts.

Change to 4 mm (US 6) needles.

Beg with a K row, work in striped st st as given for Back as folls:

Work 15 [19: 23: 27] rows, ending with stripe row 3 and **WS** facing for next row.

Place Pocket

Keeping stripes correct throughout, work as folls:

Next row (WS): P3 [4: 5: 6], cast off next 12 [13: 14: 15] sts **knitwise** (for pocket opening), P to end.

Next row (RS): K8 [9: 9: 10], with RS facing K across 12 [13: 14: 15] sts of second Pocket Lining, K to end. 23 [26: 28: 31] sts.

Cont in striped st st until Right Front meas 22 [30: 34: 38] rows less than Back to start of shoulder shaping, ending with RS facing for next row.

Shape Front Neck Slope

Keeping stripes correct, work as folls:

Next row (RS): K2, sl 1, K1, psso, K to end. 22 [25: 27: 30] sts.

Working all neck decreases as set by last row, dec 1 st at neck edge of 2nd and every foll 4th row until 17 [18: 19: 21] sts rem.

Work 4 rows, ending with **WS** facing for next row.

Shape Shoulder

Keeping stripes correct, cast off 9 [9: 10: 11] sts at beg of next row.

Work 1 row.

Cast off rem 8 [9: 9: 10] sts.

SLEEVES

Using 3.25 mm (US 3) needles and yarn **A** cast on 34 [38: 38: 42] sts.

Work in rib as given for Back for 9 [9: 11: 11] rows, ending with **WS** facing for next row.

Next row (WS): Rib 4 [3: 6: 5], work 2 tog, (rib 6 [4: 6: 4], work 2 tog) 3 [5: 3: 5] times, rib 4 [3: 6: 5]. 30 [32: 34: 36] sts.

Change to 4 mm (US 6) needles.

Beg with a K row, work in striped st st as given for Back as folls:

Work 2 rows, ending with RS facing for next row.

Next row (RS): K2, M1, K to last 2 sts, M1, K2. 32 [34: 36: 38] sts.

Working all increases as set by last row, inc 1 st at each end of every foll 4th row until there are 44 [48: 54: 60] sts.

Cont straight until Sleeve meas 15 [17: 20: 24] cm (6 [6½: 8: 9½]in), ending with RS facing for next row.

Shape Top

Keeping stripes correct, cast off 5 [5: 6: 7] sts at beg of next 6 [4: 6: 4] rows, then - [6: -: 6] sts at beg of next 2 rows.

Cast off rem 14 [16: 18: 20] sts.

MAKING UP

Join both shoulder seams.

Front Borders and Collar

With RS facing and using 3.25 mm (US 3) circular needle and yarn **A**, beg and ending at front cast-on edges, pick up and knit 51 [55: 60: 75] sts evenly up straight edge to start of front neck slope, 30 [33: 37: 38] sts evenly along front neck slope edge to shoulder seam, K across 17 [21: 23: 25] sts on back holder inc 1 [0: 0: 1] st at centre, then pick up and knit 30 [33: 37: 38] sts evenly down front neck slope edge, 51 [55: 60: 75] sts evenly along straight edge to cast-on edge. 180 [197: 217: 252] sts.

Work back and forth in rows not rounds, work as folls:

Row 1 (WS): K1, (P2, K2) 13 [14: 15: 19] times, (P2, inc knitwise into next st) 24 [27: 31: 32] times, P2, (K2, P2) 13 [14: 15: 19] times, K1. 204 [224: 248: 284] sts.

Row 2: K3, *P2, K2, rep from * to last st, K1.

Last row sets the sts - first and last st of every row worked as a K st with all other sts in rib.

Keeping rib correct, cont as folls:

Row 3: Rib 114 [126: 139: 159], wrap next st (by slipping next st from left needle onto right needle, taking yarn to opposite side of work between needles and then slipping same st back onto left needle - when working back across wrapped sts work the wrapped st and the wrapping loop tog as one st) and turn.

Row 4: Rib 24 [28: 30: 34], wrap next st and turn.

Row 5: Rib 27 [31: 33: 37], wrap next st and turn.

Row 6: Rib 30 [34: 36: 40], wrap next st and turn.

Cont in this way, working **3 more** sts on every row before wrapping next st and turning, until the foll row has been worked:

Next row (RS): Rib 96 [112: 126: 130], wrap next st and turn.

Next row (WS): Rib to end.

Now working across **all** sts, cont as folls:

Next row (RS): Rib to last 49 [53: 57: 70] sts, *yo, work 2 tog (to make a buttonhole), rib 9 [10: 11: 11], rep from * 3 [3: 3: 4] times more, yo, work 2 tog

(to make 5th [5th: 5th: 6th] buttonhole), rib 3.

Work 3 rows in rib, ending with RS facing for next row.

Cast off in rib.

Mark points along side seam edges of back and fronts 11 [12: 13:14] cm (4¼ [4¾: 5¼: 5½] in) either side of shoulder seams, then sew shaped cast-off edges of sleeves to back and fronts between these points. Join side and sleeve seams. Slip stitch pocket linings in place to WS. Sew on buttons to correspond with buttonholes.

Pin out garment to measurements given and cover with damp cloths and leave to dry naturally. See ball band for washing and further care instructions.

29

SKILL LEVEL

AMANTA

SIZE

AGE	0-6 months	6-12 months	1-2 years	2-3 years
To fit chest				
	41	46	51	56 cm
	16	18	20	22 in
Actual chest measurement				
	45	51	56	62 cm
	17¾	20	22	24½ in
Full length, from shoulder				
	21	25	29	35 cm
	8¼	9¾	11½	13¾ in
Sleeve length				
	15	17	20	24 cm
	6	6½	8	9½ in

YARN

Jody Long Ciao

3 [3: 4: 4] x 50g balls in Wisteria 018

NEEDLES

1 pair 3.25 mm (no 10) (US 3) needles
1 pair 4 mm (no 8) (US 6) needles

BUTTONS - 1 [1: 1: 1]

TENSION

22 sts and 30 rows to 10 cm (4 in) measured over st st using 4 mm (US 6) needles.

ABBREVIATIONS

See inside front flap

BACK

Using 3.25 mm (US 3) needles cast on 58 [64: 70: 76] sts.
Work in g st for 4 [4: 6: 6] rows, ending with RS facing for next row.
Change to 4 mm (US 6) needles.
Beg with a K row, work in st st as folls:
Work 2 rows, ending with RS facing for next row.
Dec 1 st at each end of next row, then on 3 [2: 1: 3] foll 4th [6th: 8th: 14th] rows, then on - [1: 2: -] foll - [8th: 10th: -] rows. 50 [56: 62: 68] sts.
Cont in st st until Back meas 9 [12: 15: 20] cm (3½ [4¾: 6: 8] in), ending with RS facing for next row.

Shape Raglan Armholes

Cast off 4 sts at beg of next 2 rows. 42 [48: 54: 60] sts.

0-6 Months and 6-12 Months Only

Dec 1 st at each end of next and foll 4th row. 38 [44] sts.
Work 3 rows straight, ending with RS facing for next row.

1-2 Years Only

Dec 1 st at each end of next row. [52] sts.
Work 3 rows straight, ending with RS facing for next row.

2-3 Years Only

Dec 1 st at each end of next 2 rows, ending with RS facing for next row. [56] sts.

All Sizes

Dec 1 st at each end of next and 1 [2: 5: 7] foll alt rows.
Work 1 row, ending with RS facing for next row.
Cast off rem 34 [38: 40: 40] sts **loosely.**

LEFT FRONT

Using 3.25 mm (US 3) needles cast on 35 [38: 43: 46] sts.

Work in g st for 3 [3: 5: 5] rows, ending with **WS** facing for next row.

Next row (WS): K11 [11: 13: 13] sts, slip these 11 [11: 13: 13] sts on a holder (for Button Band), K to end. 24 [27: 30: 33] sts.

Change to 4 mm (US 6) needles.

Beg with a K row, work in st st as folls:

Work 2 rows, ending with RS facing for next row.

Dec 1 st at beg of next row, then on 3 [2: 1: 3] foll 4th [6th: 8th:14th] rows, then on - [1: 2: -] foll - [8th: 10th: -] rows. 20 [23: 26: 29] sts.

Cont in st st until Left Front matches Back to beg of raglan armhole shaping, ending with RS facing for next row.

Shape Raglan Armholes

Cast off 4 sts at beg of next row. 16 [19: 22: 25] sts.

Work 1 row.

0-6 Months, 6-12 Months and 1-2 Years Only

Dec 1 st at raglan edge of next and 2 [1: 1] foll 4th rows. 13 [17:20]sts.

Work 0 [3: 1] rows straight, ending with **WS** [RS: RS] facing for next row.

2-3 Years Only

Dec 1 st at raglan edge of next 2 rows, ending with RS facing for next row. 23 sts.

6-12 Months, 1-2 Years and 2-3 Years Only

Dec 1 st at raglan edge of next and [1: 3: 5] foll alt rows, ending with **WS** facing for next row. [15: 16: 17] sts.

All Sizes
Shape Front Neck

Next row (WS): Cast off 9 [11: 12: 6] sts, P to end. 4 [4: 4: 11] sts.

2-3 Years Only

Dec 1 st at each end of next row. 9 sts.

Next row (WS): Cast off 5 sts, P to end. 4 sts.

All Sizes

Next row (RS): (K2tog) twice. 2 sts.

Next row: P2tog. Fasten off.

RIGHT FRONT

Using 3.25 mm (US 3) needles cast on 35 [38: 43: 46] sts.

Work in g st for 3 [3: 5: 5] rows, ending with **WS** facing for next row.

Next row (WS): K24 [27: 30: 33] sts and turn, leaving rem 11 [11: 13: 13] sts on a holder (for Buttonhole Band). 24 [27: 30: 33] sts.

Change to 4 mm (US 6) needles.

Beg with a K row, work in st st as folls:

Work 2 rows, ending with RS facing for next row.

Dec 1 st at end of next row, then on 3 [2: 1: 3] foll 4th [6th: 8th: 14th] rows, then on - [1: 2: -] foll - [8th: 10th: -] rows. 20 [23: 26:29] sts.

Cont in st st until Right Front matches Back to beg of raglan armhole shaping, ending with RS facing for next row.

Shape Raglan Armholes

Work 1 row.

Cast off 4 sts at beg of next row. 16 [19: 22: 25] sts.

0-6 Months, 6-12 Months and 1-2 Years Only

Dec 1 st at raglan edge of next and 1 [2: 1] foll 4th rows. 14 [16:20]sts.

Work 3 [1: 1] rows straight, ending with RS facing for next row.

2-3 Years Only

Dec 1 st at raglan edge of next 2 rows, ending with RS facing for next row. 23 sts.

1-2 Years and 2-3 Years Only

Dec 1 st at raglan edge of next and [2: 4] foll alt rows.

Work 1 row, ending with RS facing for next row.

All Sizes
Shape Front Neck

Next row (RS): Cast off 9 [11: 12: 6] sts, K to last 2 sts, K2tog. 4 [4: 4: 11] sts.

Work 1 [1: 1: 0] rows, ending with RS [RS: RS: **WS**] facing for next row.

2-3 Years Only

Dec 1 st at each end of next row. 9 sts.

Next row (RS): Cast off 5 sts, P to end. 4 sts.

Work 1 row.

All Sizes

Next row (RS): (K2tog) twice. 2 sts.

Next row: P2tog. Fasten off.

SLEEVES

Using 3.25 mm (US 3) needles cast on 34 [36: 38: 38] sts.

Work in g st for 4 [4: 6: 6] rows, ending with RS facing for next row.

Change to 4 mm (US 6) needles.

Beg with a K row, work in st st as folls:

Inc 1 st at each end of 11th [11th: 13th: 13th] row, then on 2 [1: 2: 4] foll 10th [6th: 6th: 6th] rows, then on - [2: 2: 2] foll - [8th: 8th: 8th] rows. 40 [44: 48: 52] sts.

Cont straight until Sleeve meas 15 [17: 20: 24] cm (6 [6¾: 8: 9½]in), ending with RS facing for next row.

Shape Raglans

Cast off 4 sts at beg of next 2 rows. 32 [36: 40: 44] sts.

Dec 1 st at each end of next and 2 [2: 2: 1] foll 4th rows, then on 1 [2: 3: 6] foll alt rows. 24 [26: 28: 28] sts.

Work 1 row, ending with RS facing for next row.

Cast off **loosely**.

MAKING UP

Button Band

With RS facing, using 3.25 mm (US 3) needles cast on 1 st (this st will be used for sewing the band to left front opening edge), knit across 11 [11: 13: 13] sts from Button Band holder. 12 [12: 14: 14]sts.

Cont working in g st until band is of sufficient length to go up left front opening edge to start of neck shaping when slightly stretched, ending with RS facing for next row.

Break off yarn and slip these 12 [12: 14: 14] sts on a holder (for Yoke).

Buttonhole Band

With **WS** facing, using 3.25 mm (US 3) needles cast on 1 st (this st will be used for sewing the band to right front opening edge), knit across 11 [11: 13: 13] sts from Buttonhole Band holder. 12 [12: 14: 14] sts.

Cont working in g st until band is of sufficient length to go up right front opening edge to start of neck shaping when slightly stretched, ending with RS facing for next row.

Do not break yarn.

Yoke

Join raglan seams.

With RS facing, using 3.25 mm (US 3) needles work across 12 [12: 14: 14] sts of buttonhole band as folls: K10 [10: 12: 12], K2tog, pick up and knit 11 [13: 14: 14] sts evenly up right front neck, 21 [23: 25: 25] sts from 24 [26: 28: 28] sts cast off at top of right sleeve, 30 [34: 36: 36] sts from 34 [38: 40: 40] sts cast off at back, 21 [23: 25: 25] sts from 24 [26: 28: 28] sts cast off at top of left sleeve, 11 [13: 14: 14] sts evenly down left front neck, then work across 12 [12: 14: 14] sts of button band as folls: K2tog, K10 [10: 12: 12]. 116 [128: 140: 140] sts.

Working entirely in g st, work as folls:

Work 5 rows, ending with RS facing for next row.

Next row (RS): K15 [12: 18: 18], K2tog, (K4, K2tog) 14 [17: 17: 17] times, K15 [12: 18: 18]. 101 [110: 122: 122] sts.

Work 5 rows.

Next row (RS): K5, cast off 2 sts (for buttonhole), K6 [4: 10: 10], K2tog, (K3, K2tog) 14 [17: 17: 17] times, K15 [11: 17: 17]. 84 [90: 102: 102] sts.

Next row: K to last 5 sts, cast on 2 sts (for buttonhole, K5. 86 [92: 104: 104] sts.

Work 4 rows.

Next row (RS): K14 [11: 17: 17], K2tog, (K2, K2tog) 14 [17: 17: 17] times, K14 [11: 17: 17]. 71 [74: 86: 86] sts.

Work 4 [4: 6: 6] rows, ending with **WS** facing for next row.

Cast off **knitwise** (on **WS**).

Join side and sleeve seams. Sew bands in position (using cast on st). Sew on buttons.

Pin out garment to measurements given and cover with damp cloths and leave to dry naturally. See ball band for washing and further care instructions.

AURORA

SIZE

AGE	0-6 months	6-12 months	1-2 years	2-3 years
To fit chest				
	41	46	51	56 cm
	16	18	20	22 in
Actual chest measurement				
	45	49	55	60 cm
	17¾	19¼	21¾	23¾ in
Full length, from shoulder				
	22	25	28	31 cm
	8¾	9¾	11	12 in
Sleeve length				
	15	17	20	24 cm
	6	6½	8	9½ in

YARN

Jody Long Ciao
3 [4: 4: 5] x 50g balls in Wisteria 018

NEEDLES

1 pair 3.25 mm (no 10) (US 3) needles
1 pair 4 mm (no 8) (US 6) needles
4 mm (no 8) (US 6) circular needle

BUTTONS - 3 [3: 3: 3]

TENSION

22 sts and 30 rows to 10 cm (4 in) measured st st, 26 sts and 32 rows to 10 cm (4 in) measured over patt, both using 4 mm (US 6) needles.

ABBREVIATIONS

See inside front flap

BODY (Worked in one piece to armholes)

Using 4 mm (US 6) circular needle cast on 176 [188: 200: 248] sts.
Working back and forth in rows not rounds, work as folls:
Row 1 (RS): K4, *(K2tog) twice, (yo, K1) 4 times, (sl 1, K1, psso) twice, rep from * to last 4 sts, K4.
Row 2: K4, P to last 4 sts, K4.
Rows 3 and 4: As rows 1 and 2.
Rows 5 and 6: Knit.
These 6 rows form patt.
Work a further 23 [29: 35: 41] rows, ending with **WS** facing for next row.
Next row (WS): K4, P0 [4: 2: 0], (P2tog) 0 [12: 6: 0] times, P0 [2: 2: 0], *P2 [2: 2: 1], (P2tog) 12 [13: 8: 14] times, P2 [2: 2: 1], rep from * to last 4 [34: 20: 4] sts, P0 [2: 2: 0], (P2tog) 0 [12: 6: 0] times, P0 [4: 2: 0], K4. 104 [112: 124: 136] sts.
Work 2 rows in g st, ending with RS facing for next row.
Next row (RS): K2, yo, K2tog (to make a buttonhole), K to end.
Next row: Knit.
Next row: K4 and slip these sts onto a holder (for Buttonhole Band), K to last 4 sts and turn, slip rem 4 sts onto another holder (for Button Band). 96 [104: 116: 128] sts.
Beg with a P row, work in st st across **all** sts as folls:
Work 3 [3: 5: 5] rows, ending with RS facing for next row.

Divide For Armholes

Next row (RS): Knit 23 [25: 28: 31] sts and slip these sts onto a holder (for right front), knit 50 [54: 60: 66] sts and turn, leaving rem 23 [25: 28: 31] sts on another holder (for left front).
Working on this set of 50 [54: 60: 66] sts only for Back section as folls:
Work 1 row, ending with RS facing for next row.
Dec 1 st at each end of next 5 [5: 5: 6] rows. 40 [44: 50: 54] sts.

Cont straight until armhole meas 10 [11: 12: 13] cm (4 [4¼: 4¾: 5] in), ending with RS facing for next row.

Shape Shoulders

Cast off 5 [6: 7: 8] sts at beg of next 2 rows, then 6 [6: 7: 8] sts at beg of foll 2 rows.

Break yarn and leave rem 18 [20: 22: 22] sts on a holder (for Neckband).

Shape Left Front

Slip 23 [25: 28: 31] sts on left front holder onto 4 mm (US 6) needles and rejoin yarn with RS facing.

Now work as folls:

Work 2 rows, ending with RS facing for next row.

Dec 1 st at armhole edge of next 5 [5: 5: 6] rows. 18 [20: 23: 25] sts. Cont straight until 12 [14: 16: 16] rows less have been worked than on Back to beg of shoulder shaping, ending with RS facing for next row.

Shape Front Neck

Work 1 row.

Next row (WS): Cast off 3 [4: 5: 5] sts, P to end. 15 [16: 18: 20] sts.

Dec 1 st at neck edge of next and 3 foll alt rows. 11 [12: 14: 16] sts. Work 3 [5: 7: 7] rows, ending with RS facing for next row.

Shape Shoulder

Cast off 5 [6: 7: 8] sts at beg of next row.

Work 1 row.

Cast off rem 6 [6: 7: 8] sts.

Shape Right Front

Slip 23 [25: 28: 31] sts on right front holder onto 4 mm (US 6) needles and rejoin yarn with **WS** facing.

Now work as folls:

Work 1 row, ending with RS facing for next row.

Dec 1 st at armhole edge of next 5 [5: 5: 6] rows. 18 [20: 23: 25] sts. Cont straight until 12 [14: 16: 16] rows less have been worked than on Back to beg of shoulder shaping, ending with RS facing for next row.

Shape Front Neck

Next row (RS): Cast off 3 [4: 5: 5] sts, K to end. 15 [16: 18: 20] sts. Work 1 row.

Dec 1 st at neck edge of next and 3 foll alt rows. 11 [12: 14: 16] sts. Work 4 [6: 8: 8] rows, ending with **WS** facing for next row.

Shape Shoulder

Cast off 5 [6: 7: 8] sts at beg of next row.

Work 1 row.

Cast off rem 6 [6: 7: 8] sts.

SLEEVES

Using 3.25 mm (US 3) needles cast on 26 [28: 30: 32] sts.

Work 4 rows in g st, ending with RS facing for next row.

Change to 4 mm (US 6) needles.

Beg with a K row, work in st st as folls:

Inc 1 st at each end of 3rd and every foll 4th [4th: 4th: 6th] row until there are 34 [34: 34: 46] sts, then on 3 [5: 7: 3] foll 6th [6th: 6th: 8th] rows. 40 [44: 48: 52] sts.

Cont straight until Sleeve meas 15 [17: 20: 24] cm (6 [6¾: 8: 9½] in), ending with RS facing for next row.

Shape Top

Place markers at both ends of last row (to denote top of sleeve seam).

Dec 1 st at each end of next 5 [5: 5: 6] rows. 30 [34: 38: 40] sts.

Work 1 [1: 1: 0] rows, ending with RS facing for next row.

Cast off 3 [4: 4: 5] sts at beg of next 4 rows, then 3 [3: 5: 4] sts at beg of foll 2 rows.

Cast off rem 12 sts.

Front

Back

MAKING UP

Button Band

Using 4 mm (US 6) needles cast on 1 st (this first st will be used for sewing the border to left front opening edge), with RS facing, K across 4 sts left on a holder (for Button Band). 5 sts.

Cont in g st until the button band is long enough to reach the start of neck shaping when slightly stretched, ending with RS facing for next row.

Slip these 5 sts onto a holder (for Neckband).

Mark positions for 3 buttons the first one to be on 2nd row below sts left on stitch holder and the last one in 3rd of 4 rows g st corresponding to buttonhole already worked on Right Front, the rem 1 evenly spaced between these two.

Buttonhole Band

Using 4 mm (US 6) needles cast on 1 st (this last st will be used for sewing the border to right front opening edge), with **WS** facing, K across 4 sts left on a holder (for Buttonhole Band). 5 sts.

Cont in g st until buttonhole band meas exactly the same as button band working 2 buttonholes as before (on RS rows) to correspond with 1st and 2nd markers on button band, ending with RS facing for next row.

Slip these 5 sts onto a holder (for Neckband).

Do not break yarn.

Neckband

Join both shoulder seams.

With RS facing, using 4 mm (US 6) needles, work across the 5 sts of buttonhole band as folls: K3, K2tog, pick up and knit 15 [16: 17: 19] sts up right side of front neck, K across 18 [20: 22: 22] sts on back holder, pick up and knit 15 [16: 17: 19] sts down left side of front neck, then work across the 5 sts of button band from holder as folls: K2tog, K3. 56 [60: 64: 68] sts.

Work in g st for 2 rows, ending with WS facing for next row.

Cast off **knitwise** (on **WS**).

Join sleeve seams. Sew sleeves into armholes. Slip stitch front bands to corresponding front opening edge. Sew on buttons.

Pin out garment to measurements given and cover with damp cloths, and leave to dry naturally, taking care not to flatten the Roses. See ball band for washing and further care instructions.

BAMBINA

SIZE

AGE	0-6 months	6-12 months	1-2 years	2-3 years
To fit chest				
	41	46	51	56 cm
	16	18	20	22 in
Actual chest measurement				
	43	48	54	57 cm
	17	19	21¼	22½ in
Full length, from back neck				
	32	36	40	46 cm
	12½	14	15¾	18 in

YARN

Jody Long Ciao
3 [4: 4: 5] x 50g balls in Wisteria 018

NEEDLES

1 pair 3.25 mm (no 10) (US 3) needles
1 pair 4 mm (no 8) (US 6) needles

TENSION

22 sts and 30 rows to 10 cm (4 in) measured over st st using 4 mm (US 6) needles.

ABBREVIATIONS

See inside front flap

SPECIAL ABBREVIATION

MB = make bobble as folls: K into front, back and front again of next st, turn, P3, turn, K3, turn, P1, P2tog, turn, K2tog. – bobble complete.

BACK

Using 3.25 mm (US 3) needles cast on 79 [83: 91: 99] sts.
Row 1 (RS): K1, *yo, K2tog, rep from * to end.
Work 3 [3: 5: 5] rows in g st, ending with RS facing or next row.
Change to 4 mm (US 6) needles.
Now work in patt as folls:
Row 1 (RS): P2 [4: 5: 6], work across next 15 sts as row 1 of chart, *P5 [5: 7: 9], work across next 15 sts as row 1 of chart, rep from * to last 2 [4: 5: 6] sts, P2 [4: 5: 6].
Row 2: K2 [4: 5: 6], work across next 15 sts as row 2 of chart, *K5 [5: 7: 9], work across next 15 sts as row 2 of chart, rep from * to last 2 [4: 5: 6] sts, K2 [4: 5: 6].
Last 2 rows set position of charts with 5 [5: 7: 9] sts of reverse st st between the charts and 2 [4: 5: 6] sts at either end.
Cont as set until all 29 rows of chart have been completed, ending with **WS** facing for next row.
Next row (WS): Knit.
Change to 3.25 mm (US 3) needles.
Work 4 rows in g st, ending with RS facing for next row.
Change to 4 mm (US 6) needles.
Beg with a K row, work in st st until Back meas 21 [23: 25: 30] cm (8¼ [9: 9¾: 11¾] in), ending with **WS** facing for next row.
Next row (WS): P3, (P2tog) 12 [7: 6: 8] times, (P1, P2tog) 8[16:20:20]times,P1,(P2tog)12[7:6:8]times,P3. 47[53:59:63] sts.
Now work bodice as folls:
Row 1 (RS): K1, *P1, K1, rep from * to end.
Row 2: As row 1.
These 2 rows form moss st.
Cont in moss st for a further 8 [8: 12: 12] rows, ending with RS facing for next row.

Shape Armholes

Keeping patt correct, cast off 4 [4: 5: 5] sts at beg of next 2 rows. 39 [45: 49: 53] sts. **

Dec 1 st at each end of next 3 [5: 5: 5] rows, then on 1 [1: 2: 3] foll alt rows. 31 [33: 35: 37] sts.

Cont straight until armhole meas 5 [7: 8: 9] cm (2 [2¾: 3: 3½] in), ending with RS facing for next row.

Shape Back Neck

Next row (RS): Patt 12 [12: 12: 13] and turn, leaving rem sts on a holder.

Work on this set of 12 [12: 12: 13] sts only for first side of neck as folls:

Keeping patt correct, dec 1 st at neck edge of next 2 rows, then on 2 foll alt rows.

Work 3 rows, ending with RS facing for next row.

Cast off rem 8 [8: 8: 9] sts in patt.

Return to sts left on a holder and slip centre 7 [9: 11: 11] sts onto another holder (for Neckband). Rejoin yarn to rem sts with RS facing, patt to end. 12 [12: 12: 13] sts.

Keeping patt correct, dec 1 st at neck edge of next 2 rows, then on 2 foll alt rows.

Work 3 rows, ending with RS facing for next row.

Cast off rem 8 [8: 8: 9] sts in patt.

FRONT

Work as given for Back to **.

Shape Armholes

Dec 1 st at each end of next 2 [4: 4: 4] rows, ending with RS facing for next row. 35 [37: 41: 45] sts.

6-12 Months, 1-2 Years and 2-3 Years Only

Dec 1 st at each end of next and [1: 2: 2] foll alt rows. [33: 35: 39] sts.

Work [3: 3: 1] rows, ending with RS facing for next row.

All Sizes
Shape Neck

Next row (RS): (Patt 2 tog) 1 [0: 0: 1] time, patt until there are 13 [12: 12: 13] sts on right needle and turn, leaving rem sts on a holder.

Work on this set of 13 [12: 12: 13] sts only for first side of neck as folls:

Next row: Patt 2 tog, patt to end. 12 [11: 11: 12] sts.

0-6 Months Only

Next row (RS): Patt 2 tog, patt to last 2 sts, patt 2 tog. 10 sts.

6-12 Months, 1-2 Years and 2-3 Years Only

Dec 1 st at neck edge of next row. [10: 10: 11] sts.

All Sizes

Work 1 row, ending with RS facing for next row.

Dec 1 st at neck edge of next and foll 4th row. 8 [8: 8: 9] sts.

Cont straight until armhole meas same as Back armhole, ending with RS facing for next row.

Cast off in patt.

Return to sts left on a holder and slip centre 7 [9: 11: 11] sts onto another holder (for Neckband). Rejoin yarn to rem sts with RS facing, patt to last 2 [0: 0: 2] sts, (patt 2 tog) 1 [0: 0: 1] time. 13 [12: 12: 13] sts.

Next row (WS): Patt to last 2 sts, patt 2 tog. 12 [11: 11: 12] sts.

0-6 Months Only

Next row (RS): Patt 2 tog, patt to last 2 sts, patt 2 tog. 10 sts.

6-12 Months, 1-2 Years and 2-3 Years Only

Dec 1 st at neck edge of next row. [10: 10: 11] sts.

All Sizes

Work 1 row, ending with RS facing for next row.

Dec 1 st at neck edge of next and foll 4th row. 8 [8: 8: 9] sts.

Cont straight until armhole meas same as Back armhole, ending with RS facing for next row.

Cast off in patt.

MAKING UP

Join right shoulder seam.

Neckband

With RS facing, using 3.25 mm (US 3) needles, pick up and knit 17 [18: 18: 23] sts down left side of front neck, K across 7 [9: 11: 11] sts on front holder, pick up and knit 17 [18: 18: 23] sts up right side of front neck, pick up and knit 8 [8: 9: 9] sts down right side of back neck, K across 7 [9: 11: 11] sts from back holder inc 1 st at centre, then pick up and knit 8 [8: 9: 9] sts up left side of back neck. 65 [71: 77: 87] sts.

Work 3 rows in g st, ending with RS facing for next row.

Next row (RS): K1, *yo, K2tog, rep from * to end.

Cast off **knitwise** (on **WS**).

Armhole Borders

Join left shoulder and neckband seams.

With RS facing, using 3.25 mm (US 3) needles, pick up and knit 37 [45: 49: 53] sts evenly all round armhole.

Work 3 rows in g st, ending with RS facing for next row.

Next row (RS): K1, *yo, K2tog, rep from * to end.

Cast off **knitwise** (on **WS**).

Join side and armhole border seams.

Pin out garment to measurements given and cover with damp cloths and leave to dry naturally. See ball band for washing and further care instructions.

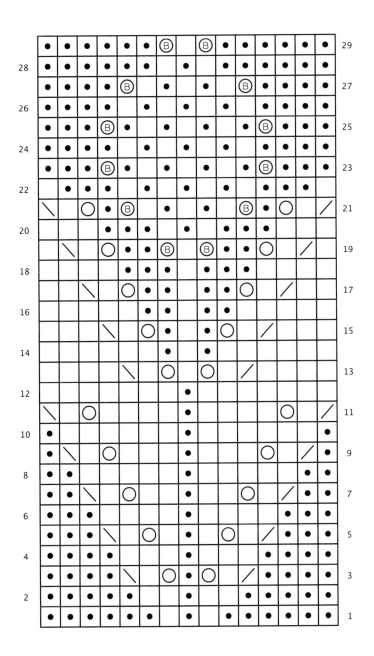

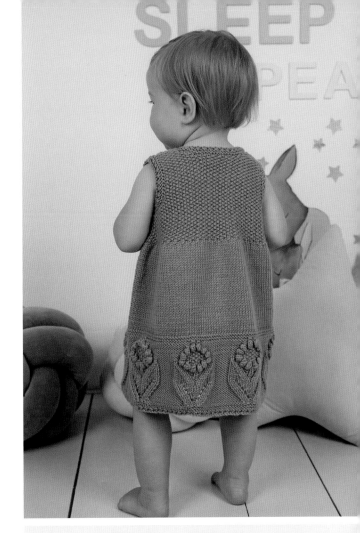

Key

☐	K on RS, P on WS	╱	K2tog
●	P on RS, K on WS	╲	sl 1, K1, psso
○	yo	Ⓑ	MB

BRUNO

SIZE

AGE	0-6 months	6-12 months	1-2 years	2-3 years
To fit chest				
	41	46	51	56 cm
	16	18	20	22 in
Actual chest measurement				
	46	52	57	63 cm
	18	20½	22½	24¾ in
Full length, from shoulder				
	24	28	32	38 cm
	9½	11	12½	15 in
Sleeve length				
	15	17	20	24 cm
	6	6½	8	9½ in

YARN

Jody Long Ciao
A 1 [1: 1: 1] x 50g balls in Rage 013
B 2 [2: 3: 3] x 50g balls in Marine 008
C 1 [1: 2: 2] x 50g balls in Alabaster 002

NEEDLES

1 pair 3.25 mm (no 10) (US 3) needles
1 pair 4 mm (no 8) (US 6) needles

BUTTONS - 2 [2: 0: 0]

TENSION

22 sts and 30 rows to 10 cm (4 in) measured over st st using 4 mm (US 6) needles.

ABBREVIATIONS

See inside front flap

CHART NOTE

Chart is worked in st st – work odd numbered rows as RS (K) rows and even numbered rows as WS (P) rows. Use a separate ball of yarn for each block of colour, twisting yarns tog on WS where they meet (to avoid holes forming).

BACK

Using 3.25 mm (US 3) needles and yarn **A** cast on 51 [57: 63: 69 sts.
Work in g st for 6 [6: 8: 8] rows, ending with RS facing for next row. Break off yarn **A**.
Change to 4 mm (US 6) needles.
Join in yarn **B**.
Beg with a K row, work 4 rows in st st, ending with RS facing for next row.
Now place chart (see chart note) as folls:
Row 1 (RS): Using yarn **B**, K4 [6: 2: 5], work next 11 sts as row 1 of chart, (using yarn **B**, K5 [6: 5: 5], work next 11 sts as row 1 of chart) 2 [2: 3: 3] times, using yarn **B**, K4 [6: 2: 5].
Row 2: Using yarn **B**, P4 [6: 2: 5], work next 11 sts as row 2 of chart, (using yarn **B**, P5 [6: 5: 5], work next 11 sts as row 2 of chart) 2 [2: 3: 3] times, using yarn **B**, P4 [6: 2: 5].
These 2 rows set the position of charts with 5 [6: 5: 5] sts between them and 4 [6: 2: 5] sts at either end of row.
Keeping patt correct, working appropriate rows of chart until all 16 rows have been completed, ending with RS facing for next row.
Beg with a K row, work in striped st st as folls:
Using yarn **B** work 4 rows.
Using yarn **C** work 2 rows.
These 6 rows form striped st st.

Cont in striped st st until Back meas 14 [17: 20: 25] cm (5½ [6¾: 8: 9¾] in), ending with RS facing for next row.

Shape Armholes
Keeping stripes correct, cast off 3 sts at beg of next 2 rows. 45 [51: 57: 63] sts.
Dec 1 st at each end of next 1 [3: 3: 5] rows, then on foll 3 [2: 3: 2] alt rows. 37 [41: 45: 49] sts.
Cont straight until armhole meas 10 [11: 12: 13] cm (4 [4¼: 4¾: 5] in), ending with RS facing for next row.

Shape Shoulders
Cast off 4 [4: 5: 5] sts at beg of next 2 rows, then 4 [5: 5: 6] sts at beg of foll 2 rows.
Break yarn and leave rem 21 [23: 25: 27] sts on a holder (for Neckband).

FRONT
Work as given for Back until Front meas 12 [14: 16: 16] rows less have been worked than on Back to start of shoulder shaping, ending with RS facing for next row.

Shape Front Neck
Keeping stripes correct, K14 [16: 18: 19] and turn, leaving rem sts on a holder.
Dec 1 st at neck edge of next 4 rows, then on foll 2 [3: 4: 4] alt rows. 8 [9: 10: 11] sts.
Work 1 [1: 3: 3] rows, ending with RS facing for next row. (**Note:** For 1st and 2nd sizes, this shoulder edge is 2 rows lower than right shoulder as the buttonhole border will be added.)

Shape Shoulder
Cast off 4 [4: 5: 5] sts at beg of next row.
Work 1 row.
Cast off rem 4 [5: 5: 6] sts.
Return to sts on holder and slip central 9 [9: 9: 11] sts onto another holder (for Neckband). Rejoin appropriate yarn colour to rem sts and K to end. 14 [16: 18: 19] sts.
Dec 1 st at neck edge of next 4 rows, then on foll 2 [3: 4: 4] alt rows. 8 [9: 10: 11] sts.
Work 4 rows, ending with **WS** facing for next row.

Shape Shoulder
Cast off 4 [4: 5: 5] sts at beg of next row.
Work 1 row.
Cast off rem 4 [5: 5: 6] sts.

SLEEVES
Using 3.25 mm (US 3) needles and yarn **A** cast on 27 [29: 31: 33] sts.
Work in g st for 6 [6: 8: 8] rows, ending with RS facing for next row.
Break off yarn **A**.
Change to 4 mm (US 6) needles.
Join in yarns **B** and **C**.
Beg with a K row, work in striped st st, repeating the 6 row stripe patt as for Back **and at same time** inc 1 st at each end of next [3rd: 3rd: 3rd] and every foll 4th row to 43 [47: 51: 47] sts, then on 0 [0: 0: 4] foll 6th rows. 43 [47: 51: 55] sts.

Cont straight until Sleeve meas 15 [17: 20: 24] cm (6 [6¾: 8: 9½] in), ending with RS facing for next row.

Shape Top
Keeping stripes correct, cast off 3 sts at beg of next 2 rows. 37 [41: 45: 49] sts.
Dec 1 st at each end of next 3 rows, then on foll 4 [5: 6: 7] alt rows, then on foll 5 rows, ending with RS facing for next row.
Cast off rem 13 [15: 17: 19] sts.

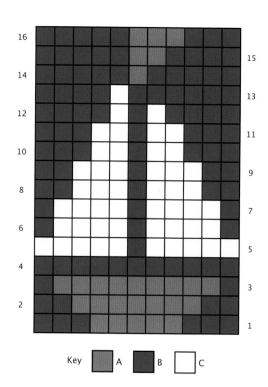

Key A B C

MAKING UP
Join right shoulder seam.

Neckband
With RS facing, using 3.25 mm (US 3) needles and yarn **A,** pick up and knit 9 [11: 15: 17] sts down left side of front neck, K across 9 [9: 9: 11] sts on front holder, pick up and knit 11 [13: 15: 17] sts up right side of front neck, then K across 21 [23: 25: 27] sts on back holder. 50 [56: 64: 72] sts.
Work in g st for 4 [4: 6: 6] rows, ending with **WS** facing for next row.
Cast off **knitwise** (on **WS**).

For 1st and 2nd Sizes Only
Back Button Border
With RS facing, using 3.25 mm (US 3) needles and yarn **A,** pick up and knit 12 [13] sts evenly across left back shoulder edge, from top of neckband to armhole edge.
Work in g st for 4 rows, ending with **WS** facing for next row.
Cast off **knitwise** (on **WS**).

Front Buttonhole Border

With RS facing, using 3.25 mm (US 3) needles and yarn **A**, pick up and knit 12 [13] sts evenly across left front shoulder edge, from armhole edge to top of neckband.

Row 1 (WS): Knit.

Row 2: K4, yo, K2tog (to make first buttonhole), K3 [4], yo, K2tog (to make 2nd buttonhole), K1.

Work in g st for a further 2 rows, ending with **WS** facing for next row.

Cast off **knitwise** (on **WS**).

Lay Front Buttonhole Border over Back Button Border so that borders overlap. Sew together at armhole edge. Attach buttons to correspond with buttonholes.

For 3rd and 4th Sizes only

Join left shoulder seam.

For All Sizes

Join side seams. Join sleeve seams. Insert sleeves into armholes. Pin out garment to measurements given, cover with damp cloths and leave to dry naturally. See ball band for washing and further care instructions.

CAPRI

SIZE

AGE	0-6 months	6-12 months	1-2 years	2-3 years
To fit chest				
	41	46	51	56 cm
	16	18	20	22 in
Actual chest measurement				
	46	52	57	63 cm
	18	20½	22½	24¾ in
Full length, from shoulder				
	24	28	32	38 cm
	9½	11	12½	15 in
Sleeve length				
	15	17	20	24 cm
	6	6½	8	9½ in

YARN
Jody Long Ciao
3 [4: 4: 5] x 50g balls in Celadon 012

NEEDLES
1 pair 3.25 mm (no 10) (US 3) needles
1 pair 4 mm (no 8) (US 6) needles

BUTTONS - 5 [5: 6: 6]

TENSION
22 sts and 30 rows to 10 cm (4 in) measured over st st using 4 mm (US 6) needles.

ABBREVIATIONS
See inside front flap

SPECIAL ABBREVIATION
MB = make bobble as folls: K into front, back, front, back and front again of next st, turn, P5, turn, K5, turn, P2tog, P1, P2tog, turn, sl 1, K2tog, psso – bobble complete.

BACK
Using 3.25 mm (US 3) needles cast on 51 [57: 63: 69] sts.
Row 1 (RS): K1, *P1, K1, rep from * to end.
Row 2: P1, *K1, P1, rep from * to end.
These 2 rows form rib.
Work in rib for a further 8 [8: 10: 10] rows, ending with RS facing for next row.
Change to 4 mm (US 6) needles.
Beg with a K row, now work in st st throughout as folls:
Cont straight until Back meas 14 [17: 20: 25] cm (5½ [6½: 8: 9¾] in), ending with RS facing for next row.

Shape Armholes
Cast off 3 sts at beg of next 2 rows. 45 [51: 57: 63] sts.
Dec 1 st at each end of next 1 [3: 3: 5] rows, then on foll 3 [2: 3: 2] alt rows. 37 [41: 45: 49] sts.
Cont straight until armhole meas 10 [11: 12: 13] cm (4 [4¼: 4¾: 5] in), ending with RS facing for next row.

Shape Shoulders
Cast off 4 [5: 5: 6] sts at beg of next 2 rows, then 5 [5: 6: 6] sts at beg of foll 2 rows.
Break yarn and leave rem 19 [21: 23: 25] sts on a holder (for Neckband).

LEFT FRONT

Using 3.25 mm (US 3) needles cast on 24 [28: 30: 34] sts.

Row 1 (RS): K1, *P1, K1, rep from * to last st, K1.

Row 2: *K1, P1, rep from * to end.

These 2 rows form rib.

Work in rib for a further 8 [8: 10: 10] rows, inc 1 [0: 1: 0] st at end of last row and ending with RS facing for next row. 25 [28: 31: 34] sts.

Change to 4 mm (US 6) needles.

Now work in patt as folls:

Row 1 (RS): Knit.

Row 2: Purl.

Row 3: K1 [4: 7: 2], (MB, K7) 3 [3: 3: 4] times.

Row 4: Purl.

Rows 5 to 8: As rows 1 and 2, twice.

Row 9: K5 [8: 3: 6], MB, (K7, MB) 2 [2: 3: 3] times, K3.

Row 10: Purl.

Rows 11 and 12: As rows 1 and 2.

These 12 rows form patt.

Cont in patt until Left Front matches Back to beg of armhole shaping, ending with RS facing for next row.

Shape Armhole

Keeping patt correct, cast off 3 sts at beg of next row. 22 [25: 28: 31] sts.

Work 1 row.

Dec 1 st at armhole edge of next 1 [3: 3: 5] rows, then on foll 3 [2: 3: 2] alt rows. 18 [20: 22: 24] sts.

Cont straight until 12 [14: 16: 16] rows less have been worked than on Back to beg of shoulder shaping, ending with RS facing for next row.

Shape Front Neck

Next row (RS): Patt 15 [17: 19: 20] sts and turn, leaving rem 3 [3: 3: 4] sts on a holder (for Neckband).

Keeping patt correct, dec 1 st at neck edge of next 4 rows, then on foll 2 [3: 4: 4] alt rows. 9 [10: 11: 12] sts.

Work 3 rows, ending with RS facing for next row.

Shape Shoulders

Cast off 4 [5: 5: 6] sts at beg of next row.

Work 1 row.

Cast off rem 5 [5: 6: 6] sts.

RIGHT FRONT

Using 3.25 mm (US 3) needles cast on 24 [28: 30: 34] sts.

Row 1 (RS): K2, *P1, K1, rep from * to end.

Row 2: *P1, K1, rep from * to end.

These 2 rows form rib.

Work in rib for a further 8 [8: 10: 10] rows, inc 1 [0: 1: 0] st at beg of last row and ending with RS facing for next row. 25 [28: 31: 34] sts.

Change to 4 mm (US 6) needles.

Now work in patt as folls:

Row 1 (RS): Knit.

Row 2: Purl.

Row 3: (K7, MB) 3 [3: 3: 4] times, K1 [4: 7: 2].

Row 4: Purl.

Rows 5 to 8: As rows 1 and 2, twice.

Row 9: K3, MB, (K7, MB) 2 [2: 3: 3] times, K5 [8: 3: 6].

Row 10: Purl.

Rows 11 and 12: As rows 1 and 2.

These 12 rows form patt.

Cont in patt until Right Front matches Back to beg of armhole shaping, ending with RS facing for next row.

Shape Armhole

Work 1 row.

Keeping patt correct, cast off 3 sts at beg of next row. 22 [25: 28: 31] sts.

Dec 1 st at armhole edge of next 1 [3: 3: 5] rows, then on foll 3 [2: 3: 2] alt rows. 18 [20: 22: 24] sts.

Cont straight until 12 [14: 16: 16] rows less have been worked than on Back to beg of shoulder shaping, ending with RS facing for next row.

Shape Front Neck

Next row (RS): K3 [3: 3: 4] and slip these sts onto a holder (for Neckband), patt to end. 15 [17: 19: 20] sts.

Keeping patt correct, dec 1 st at neck edge of next 4 rows, then on foll 2 [3: 4: 4] alt rows. 9 [10: 11: 12] sts.

Work 4 rows, ending with **WS** facing for next row.

Shape Shoulders

Cast off 4 [5: 5: 6] sts at beg of next row.

Work 1 row.

Cast off rem 5 [5: 6: 6] sts.

SLEEVES

Using 3.25 mm (US 3) needles cast on 27 [29: 31: 33] sts.

Work in rib as given for Back for 6 [6: 8: 8] rows, ending with RS facing for next row.

Change to 4 mm (US 6) needles.

Beg with a K row, now work in st st throughout as folls:

Inc 1 st at each end of next [3rd: 3rd: 3rd] and every foll 4th row until there are 43 [47: 51: 47] sts, then on 0 [0: 0: 4] foll 6th rows. 43 [47: 51: 55] sts.

Cont straight until Sleeve meas 15 [17: 20: 24] cm (6 [6¾: 8: 9½] in), ending with RS facing for next row.

Shape Top

Cast off 3 sts at beg of next 2 rows. 37 [41: 45: 49] sts.

Dec 1 st at each end of next 3 rows, then on foll 4 alt rows, then on every row until 13 sts rem, ending with RS facing for next row.

Cast off rem 13 sts.

MAKING UP

Join both shoulder seams.

Neckband

With RS facing and using 3.25 mm (US 3) needles, slip 3 [3: 3: 4] sts on right front holder onto right needle, rejoin yarn and pick up and knit 11 [13: 15: 15] sts up right side of front neck, K across 19 [21: 23: 25] sts on back holder, pick up and knit 11 [13: 15: 15] sts down left side of front neck, then K across 3 [3: 3: 4] sts on left front holder. 47 [53: 59: 63] sts.

Row 1 (WS): K1, *P1, K1, rep from * to end.

Row 2: K2, *P1, K1, rep from * to last st, K1.

These 2 rows form rib.

Cont in rib for a further 3 [3: 5: 5] rows, ending with RS facing for next row.
Cast off in rib.

Button Band

With RS facing and using 3.25 mm (US 3) needles, pick up and knit 53 [61: 71: 85] sts evenly down entire left front opening edge, from top of Neckband to cast-on edge.
Beg with row 1, work in rib as given for Neckband for 5 rows, ending with RS facing for next row.
Cast off in rib.

Buttonhole Band

With RS facing and using 3.25 mm (US 3) needles, pick up and knit 53 [61: 71: 85] sts evenly up entire right front opening edge, from cast-on edge to top of Neckband.
Beg with row 1, work in rib as given for Neckband as folls:
Work 2 rows, ending with **WS** facing for next row.
Row 3 (WS): Rib 2, *yo, work 2 tog (to make a buttonhole), rib 10 [12: 11: 14], rep from * 3 [3: 4: 4] times more, yo, work 2 tog (to make 5th [5th: 6th: 6th] buttonhole), rib 1 [1: 2: 1].
Work in rib for a further 2 rows, ending with RS facing for next row.
Cast off in rib.
Join side seams. Join sleeve seams. Sew sleeves into armholes. Sew on buttons.
Pin out garment to measurements given and cover with damp cloths and leave to dry naturally. See ball band for washing and further care instructions.

SKILL LEVEL

CARA

SIZE

AGE	0-6 months	6-12 months	1-2 years	2-3 years
To fit chest				
	41	46	51	56 cm
	16	18	20	22 in
Actual chest measurement				
	46	52	56	61 cm
	18	20½	22	24 in
Full length, from shoulder				
	21	25	29	35 cm
	8¼	9¾	11½	13¾ in
Sleeve length				
	15	17	20	24 cm
	6	6½	8	9½ in

YARN

Jody Long Ciao
4 [5: 6: 6] x 50g balls in Petal 020

NEEDLES

1 pair 3.25 mm (no 10) (US 3) needles
1 pair 4 mm (no 8) (US 6) needles

BUTTONS - 5 [5: 6: 6]

TENSION

22 sts and 30 rows to 10 cm (4 in) measured over st st using 4 mm (US 6) needles.

ABBREVIATIONS

See inside front flap

SPECIAL ABBREVIATIONS

C3B = slip next st onto cable needle and leave at back of work, K2, then K1 from cable needle.

C3F = slip next 2 sts onto cable needle and leave at front of work, K1, then K2 from cable needle.

C4B = slip next 2 sts onto cable needle and leave at back of work, K2, then K2 from cable needle.

C4F = slip next 2 sts onto cable needle and leave at front of work, K2, then K2 from cable needle.

Cr3L = slip next 2 sts onto cable needle and leave at front of work, P1, then K2 from cable needle.

Cr3R = slip next st onto cable needle and leave at back of work, K2, then P1 from cable needle.

Cr5L = slip next 2 sts onto cable needle and leave at front of work, K2, P1, then K2 from cable needle.

Cr5R = slip next 3 sts onto cable needle and leave at back of work, K2, then P1, K2 from cable needle.

MB = make bobble as folls: K into front, back and front again of next st, turn, P3, turn, K3, turn, P3, turn, sl 1, K2tog, psso - bobble complete.

Tw2B = slip next st onto cable needle and leave at back of work (RS of work), K1, then P1 tbl from cable needle.

Tw2F = slip next st onto cable needle and leave at front of work (WS of work), P1 tbl, then K1 from cable needle.

Tw2L = slip next st onto cable needle and leave at front of work, P1, then K1 tbl from cable needle.

Tw2R = slip next st onto cable needle and leave at back of work, K1 tbl, then P1 from cable needle.

BACK

Using 3.25 mm (US 3) needles cast on 63 [69: 73: 79] sts.
Row 1 (RS): K1, *P1, K1, rep from * to end.
Row 2: As row 1.
Row 3: P1, *K1, P1, rep from * to end.
Row 4: As row 3.
These 4 rows form double moss st.

Work a further 3 rows in double moss st, ending with **WS** facing for next row.

Row 8 (WS): P4 [7: 9: 12], inc **purlwise** into next st, (P3, inc **purlwise** into next st) twice, P10, inc **purlwise** into next st, P3, inc **purlwise** into next st, P10, inc **purlwise** into next st, P3, inc **purlwise** into next st, P11, inc **purlwise** into next st, P3, inc **purlwise** into next st, P4 [7: 9: 12]. 72 [78: 82: 88] sts.
Change to 4 mm (US 6) needles.

Now work in patt as folls:
Row 1 (RS): P3 [3: 5: 5], Cr3L, Cr3R, Cr3L, P12 [14: 14: 16], Cr5R, P33 [37: 37: 41], C3B, C3F, P4 [4: 6: 6].
Row 2: K4 [4: 6: 6], P6, K33 [37: 37: 41], P2, K1, P2, K12 [14: 14: 16], P2, K2, P4, K4 [4: 6: 6].
Row 3: P4 [4: 6: 6], C4B, P2, K2, P11 [13: 13: 15], Cr3R, P1, Cr3L, P15 [17: 17: 19], MB, P15 [17: 17: 19], C3B, K2, C3F, P3 [3: 5: 5].
Row 4: K3 [3: 5: 5], P8, K15 [17: 17: 19], P1 tbl, K15 [17: 17: 19], P2, K3, P2, K11 [13: 13: 15], P2, K2, P4, K4 [4: 6: 6].
Row 5: P3 [3: 5: 5], Cr3R, Cr3L, Cr3R, P10 [12: 12: 14], Cr3R, P3, Cr3L, P11 [13: 13: 15], MB, P2, K1 tbl, P2, MB, P11 [13: 13: 15], Cr3r, K4, Cr3L, P2 [2: 4: 4].
Row 6: K2 [2: 4: 4], (P2, K1, P2) twice, K11 [13: 13: 15], P1 tbl, (K2, P1 tbl) twice, K11 [13: 13: 15], P2, K5, P2, K11 [13: 13: 15], P4, K2, P2, K3 [3: 5: 5].
Row 7: P3 [3: 5: 5], K2, P2, C4F, P10 [12: 12: 14], Cr3R, P2, MB, P2, Cr3L, P8 [10: 10: 12], MB, P1, Tw2L, P1, K1 tbl, P1, Tw2R, P1, MB, P8 [10: 10: 12], Cr3R, P1, C4B, P1, Cr3L, P1 [1: 3: 3].
Row 8: K1 [1: 3: 3], (P2, K2, P2) twice, K8 [10: 10: 12], P1 tbl, K2, (P1 tbl, K1) 3 times, K1, P1 tbl, K8 [10: 10: 12], P2, K7, P2, K10 [12: 12: 14], P4, K2, P2, K3 [3: 5: 5].
Row 9: P3 [3: 5: 5], Cr3L, Cr3R, Cr3L, P9 [11: 11: 13], K2, P1, MB, P3, MB, P1, K2, P8 [10: 10: 12], Tw2L, P1, Tw2L, K1 tbl, Tw2R, P1, Tw2R, P11 [13: 13: 15], C3B, C3F, P4 [4: 6: 6].
Row 10: K4 [4: 6: 6], P6, K12 [14: 14: 16], Tw2B, K1, (P1 tbl) 3 times, K1, Tw2F, K9 [11: 11: 13], P2, K7, P2, K9 [11: 11: 13], P2, K2, P4, K4 [4: 6: 6].
Row 11: P4 [4: 6: 6], C4B, P2, K2, P9 [11: 11: 13], Cr3L, P2, MB, P2, Cr3R, P10 [12: 12: 14], Tw2L, M1P, sl 1, K2tog, psso, M1P, Tw2R, P12 [14: 14: 16], C3B, K2, C3F, P3 [3: 5: 5].
Row 12: K3 [3: 5: 5], P8, K13 [15: 15: 17], Tw2B, P1 tbl, Tw2F, K12 [14: 14: 16], P2, K5, P2, K10 [12: 12: 14], P2, K2, P4, K4 [4: 6: 6].
Row 13: P3 [3: 5: 5], Cr3R, Cr3L, Cr3R, P10 [12: 12: 14], Cr3L, P3, Cr3R, P13 [15: 15: 17], M1P, sl 1, K2tog, psso, M1P, P13 [15: 15: 17], Cr3R, K4, Cr3L, P2 [2: 4: 4].
Row 14: K2 [2: 4: 4], (P2, K1, P2) twice, K14 [16: 16: 18], P1 tbl, K15 [17: 17: 19], P2, K3, P2, K12 [14: 14: 16], P4, K2, P2, K3 [3: 5: 5].
Row 15: P3 [3: 5: 5], K2, P2, C4F, P12 [14: 14: 16], Cr3L, P1, Cr3R, P29 [33: 33: 37], Cr3R, P1, C4B, P1, Cr3L, P1 [1: 3: 3].
Row 16: K1 [1: 3: 3], (P2, K2, P2) twice, K30 [34: 34: 38], P2, K1,
P2, K13 [15: 15: 17], P4, K2, P2, K3 [3: 5: 5].
These 16 rows form patt.
Work 2 rows, ending with RS facing for next row.

Shape Waist

Keeping cable panels correct, work as folls:
Next row (RS): Patt 12 [12: 14: 14], P2tog, P5 [7: 7: 9], P2tog tbl, patt 30 [32: 32: 34], P2tog, P4 [6: 6: 8], P2tog tbl, patt 13 [13: 15: 15]. 68 [74: 78: 84] sts.
Work 3 [5: 7: 11] rows.
Next row (RS): Patt 12 [12: 14: 14], P2tog, P3 [5: 5: 7], P2tog tbl, patt 30 [32: 32: 34], P2tog, P2 [4: 4: 6], P2tog tbl, patt 13 [13: 15: 15]. 64 [70: 74: 80] sts.
Work 3 [5: 7: 11] rows.
Next row (RS): Patt 12 [12: 14: 14], P2tog, P1 [3: 3: 5], P2tog tbl, patt 30 [32: 32: 34], P2tog, P0 [2: 2: 4], P2tog tbl, patt 13 [13: 15: 15]. 60 [66: 70: 76] sts.
Cont straight until Back meas 24 [28: 32: 38] cm (9½ [11: 12½: 15] in), ending with RS facing for next row.

Shape Shoulders

Keeping patt correct, cast off 10 [11: 12: 13] sts at beg of next 2 rows, then 11 [12: 12: 14] sts at beg of foll 2 rows.
Break yarn and slip rem 18 [20: 22: 22] sts on a holder (for Collar).

LEFT FRONT

Using 3.25 mm (US 3) needles cast on 39 [41: 43: 45] sts.
Work 7 rows in double moss st as given for Back, ending with **WS** facing for next row.

Row 8 (WS): Patt 6 sts, slip these 6 sts on a holder (for Button Band), P5, inc **purlwise** into next st, P3, inc **purlwise** into next st, P11, inc **purlwise** into next st, P3, inc **purlwise** into next st, P7 [9: 11: 13]. 37 [39: 41: 43] sts.
Change to 4 mm (US 6) needles.
Now work in patt as folls:
Row 1 (RS): P3 [3: 5: 5], Cr3L, Cr3R, Cr3L, P12 [14: 14: 16], Cr5R, P8.
Row 2: K8, P2, K1, P2, K12 [14: 14: 16], P2, K2, P4, K4 [4: 6: 6].
Row 3: P4 [4: 6: 6], C4B, P2, K2, P11 [13: 13: 15], Cr3R, P1, Cr3L, P7.
Row 4: K7, P2, K3, P2, K11 [13: 13: 15], P2, K2, P4, K4 [4: 6: 6].
Row 5: P3 [3: 5: 5], Cr3R, Cr3L, Cr3R, P10 [12: 12: 14], Cr3R, P3, Cr3L, P6.
Row 6: K6, P2, K5, P2, K11 [13: 13: 15], P4, K2, P2, K3 [3: 5: 5].
Row 7: P3 [3: 5: 5], K2, P2, C4F, P10 [12: 12: 14], Cr3R, P2, MB, P2, Cr3L, P5.
Row 8: K5, P2, K7, P2, K10 [12: 12: 14], P4, K2, P2, K3 [3: 5: 5].
Row 9: P3 [3: 5: 5], Cr3L, Cr3R, Cr3L, P9 [11: 11: 13], K2, P1, MB, P3, MB, P1, K2, P5.
Row 10: K5, P2, K7, P2, K9 [11: 11: 13], P2, K2, P4, K4 [4: 6: 6].
Row 11: P4 [4: 6: 6], C4B, P2, K2, P9 [11: 11: 13], Cr3L, P2, MB, P2, Cr3R, P5.
Row 12: K6, P2, K5, P2, K10 [12: 12: 14], P2, K2, P4, K4 [4: 6: 6].
Row 13: P3 [3: 5: 5], Cr3R, Cr3L, Cr3R, P10 [12: 12: 14], Cr3L, P3, Cr3R, P6.
Row 14: K7, P2, K3, P2, K12 [14: 14: 16], P4, K2, P2, K3 [3: 5: 5].
Row 15: P3 [3: 5: 5], K2, P2, C4F, P12 [14: 14: 16], Cr3L, P1, Cr3R, P7.

Row 16: K8, P2, K1, P2, K13 [15: 15: 17], P4, K2, P2, K3 [3: 5: 5]. These 16 rows form patt.

Work 2 rows, ending with RS facing for next row.

Shape Waist

Keeping cable panels correct, work as folls:

Next row (RS): Patt 12 [12: 14: 14], P2tog, P5 [7: 7: 9], P2tog tbl, patt 16. 35 [37: 39: 41] sts.

Work 3 [5: 7: 11] rows.

Next row (RS): Patt 12 [12: 14: 14], P2tog, P3 [5: 5: 7], P2tog tbl, patt 16. 33 [35: 37: 39] sts.

Work 3 [5: 7: 11] rows.

Next row (RS): Patt 12 [12: 14: 14], P2tog, P1 [3: 3: 5], P2tog tbl, patt 16. 31 [33: 35: 37] sts.

Cont straight until 10 [10: 12: 12] rows less have been worked than on Back to beg of shoulder shaping, ending with RS facing for next row.

Shape Front Neck

Work 1 row.

Next row (WS): Cast off 6 [6: 7: 6] sts, patt to end. 25 [27: 28: 31] sts.

Keeping patt correct, dec 1 st at neck edge of next 3 rows, then on foll alt row. 8 [9: 10: 11] sts.

Work 3 [3: 5: 5] rows, ending with RS facing for next row.

Shape Shoulders

Keeping patt correct, cast off 10 [11: 12: 13] sts at beg of next row.

Work 1 row.

Cast off rem 11 [12: 12: 14] sts.

RIGHT FRONT

Using 3.25 mm (US 3) needles cast on 39 [41: 43: 45] sts.

Work 4 rows in double moss st as given for Back, ending with RS facing for next row.

Row 5: Patt 2 sts, cast off next 2 sts (for buttonhole), patt to end.

Row 6: Patt to last 2 sts, cast on 2 sts (for buttonhole), patt 2.

Work 1 more row in double moss st.

Row 8 (WS): P7 [9: 11: 13], inc **purlwise** into next st, P3, inc **purlwise** into next st, P11, inc **purlwise** into next st, P3, inc **purlwise** into next st, P5, turn and slip rem 6 sts on a holder (for Buttonhole Band). 37 [39: 41: 43] sts.

Change to 4 mm (US 6) needles.

Now work in patt as folls:

Row 1 (RS): P27 [29: 29: 31], C3B, C3F, P4 [4: 6: 6].

Row 2: K4 [4: 6: 6], P6, K27 [29: 29: 31].

Row 3: P10, MB, P15 [17: 17: 19], C3B, K2, C3F, P3 [3: 5: 5].

Row 4: K3 [3: 5: 5], P8, K15 [17: 17: 19], P1 tbl, K10.

Row 5: P7, MB, P2, K1 tbl, P2, MB, P11 [13: 13: 15], Cr3R, K4, Cr3L, P2 [2: 4: 4].

Row 6: K2 [2: 4: 4], (P2, K1, P2) twice, K11 [13: 13: 15], P1 tbl, (K2, P1 tbl) twice, K7.

Row 7: P5, MB, P1, Tw2L, P1, K1 tbl, P1, Tw2R, P1, MB, P8 [10: 10: 12], Cr3R, P1, C4B, P1, Cr3L, P1 [1: 3: 3].

Row 8: K1 [1: 3: 3], (P2, K2, P2) twice, K8 [10: 10: 12], P1 tbl, K2, (P1 tbl, K1) 3 times, K1, P1 tbl, K5.

Row 9: P5, Tw2L, P1, Tw2L, K1 tbl, Tw2R, P1, Tw2R, P11 [13: 13: 15], C3B, C3F, P4 [4: 6: 6].

Row 10: K4 [4: 6: 6], P6, K12 [14: 14: 16], Tw2B, K1, (P1 tbl) 3 times, K1, Tw2F, K6.

Row 11: P7, Tw2L, M1P, sl 1, K2tog, psso, M1P, Tw2R, P12 [14: 14: 16], C3B, K2, C3F, P3 [3: 5: 5].

Row 12: K3 [3: 5: 5], P8, K13 [15: 15: 17], Tw2B, P1 tbl, Tw2F, K8.

Row 13: P9, M1P, sl 1, K2tog, psso, M1P, P13 [15: 15: 17], Cr3R, K4, Cr3L, P2 [2: 4: 4].

Row 14: K2 [2: 4: 4], (P2, K1, P2) twice, K14 [16: 16: 18], P1 tbl, K10.

Row 15: P24 [26: 26: 28], Cr3R, P1, C4B, P1, Cr3L, P1 [1: 3: 3].

Row 16: K1 [1: 3: 3], (P2, K2, P2) twice, K24 [26: 26: 28]. These 16 rows form patt.

Work 2 rows, ending with RS facing for next row.

Shape Waist

Keeping cable panels correct, work as folls:

Next row (RS): Patt 16, P2tog, P4 [6: 6: 8], P2tog tbl, patt 13 [13: 15: 15]. 35 [37: 39: 41] sts.

Work 3 [5: 7: 11] rows.

Next row (RS): Patt 16, P2tog, P2 [4: 4: 6], P2tog tbl, patt 13 [13: 15: 15]. 33 [35: 37: 39] sts.

Work 3 [5: 7: 11] rows.

Next row (RS): Patt 16, P2tog, P0 [2: 2: 4], P2tog tbl, patt 13 [13: 15: 15]. 31 [33: 35: 37] sts.

Cont straight until 10 [10: 12: 12] rows less have been worked than on Back to beg of shoulder shaping, ending with RS facing for next row.

Shape Front Neck

Next row (RS): Cast off 6 [6: 7: 6] sts, patt to end. 25 [27: 28: 31] sts.

Work 1 row.

Keeping patt correct, dec 1 st at neck edge of next 3 rows, then on foll alt row. 8 [9: 10: 11] sts.

Work 4 [4: 6: 6] rows, ending with **WS** facing for next row.

Shape Shoulders

Keeping patt correct, cast off 10 [11: 12: 13] sts at beg of next row.

Work 1 row.

Cast off rem 11 [12: 12: 14] sts.

SLEEVES
LEFT SLEEVE

Using 3.25 mm (US 3) needles cast on 37 [39: 41: 43] sts.

Work 7 rows in double moss st as given for Back, ending with **WS** facing for next row.

Row 8 (WS): P2 [3: 4: 5], inc **purlwise** into next st, P3, inc **purlwise** into next st, P7, inc **purlwise** into next st, P6, inc **purlwise** into next st, P7, inc **purlwise** into next st, P3, inc **purlwise** into next st, P3 [4: 5: 6]. 43 [45: 47: 49] sts.

Change to 4 mm (US 6) needles.

Now work in patt as folls:

Row 1 (RS): (Inc purlwise into first st) 1 [0: 0: 0] times, P2 [3: 4: 4], Cr3R, Cr3L, Cr3R, P7 [8: 8: 9], Cr5R, P7 [8: 8: 9], Cr3L, Cr3R, Cr3L, P2 [3: 4: 4], (inc purlwise into last st) 1 [0: 0: 0] times. 45 [45: 47: 49] sts.

Row 2: K4 [3: 4: 4], P2, K2, P4, K8 [9: 9: 10], P2, K1, P2, K8 [9: 9: 10], P4, K2, P2, K4 [3: 4: 4].

Row 3: P4 [3: 4: 4], K2, P2, C4F, P7 [8: 8: 9], Cr3R, P1, Cr3L, P7 [8: 8: 9], C4B, P2, K2, P4 [3: 4: 4].

Row 4: K4 [3: 4: 4], P2, K2, P4, K7 [8: 8: 9], P2, K3, P2, K7 [8: 8: 9], P4, K2, P2, K4 [3: 4: 4].

Row 5: Inc purlwise into first st, P3 [2: 3: 3], Cr3L, Cr3R, Cr3L, P5 [6: 6: 7], Cr3R, P3, Cr3L, P5 [6: 6: 7], Cr3R, Cr3L, Cr3R, P3 [2: 3: 3], inc purlwise into last st. 47 [47: 49: 51] sts.

Row 6: K6 [5: 6: 6], P4, K2, P2, K5 [6: 6: 7], P2, K5, P2, K5 [6: 6: 7], P2, K2, P4, K6 [5: 6: 6].

Row 7: P6 [5: 6: 6], C4B, P2, K2, P4 [5: 5: 6], Cr3R, P2, MB, P2, Cr3L, P4 [5: 5: 6], K2, P2, C4F, P6 [5: 6: 6].

Row 8: K6 [5: 6: 6], P4, K2, P2, K4 [5: 5: 6], P2, K7, P2, K4 [5: 5: 6], P2, K2, P4, K6 [5: 6: 6].

Row 9: (Inc purlwise into first st) 0 [1: 1: 1] times, P5 [3: 4: 4], Cr3R, Cr3L, Cr3R, P4 [5: 5: 6], K2, P1, MB, P3, MB, P1, K2, P4 [5: 5: 6], Cr3L, Cr3R, Cr3L, P5 [3: 4: 4], (inc purlwise into last st) 0 [1: 1: 1] times. 47 [49: 51: 53] sts.

Row 10: K5 [5: 6: 6], P2, K2, P4, K5 [6: 6: 7], P2, K7, P2, K5 [6: 6: 7], P4, K2, P2, K5 [5: 6: 6].

Row 11: (Inc purlwise into first st) 1 [0: 0: 0] times, P4 [5: 6: 6], K2, P2, C4F, P5 [6: 6: 7], Cr3L, P2, MB, P2, Cr3R, P5 [6: 6: 7], C4B, P2, K2, P4 [5: 6: 6], (inc purlwise into last st) 1 [0: 0: 0] times. 49 [49: 51: 53] sts.

Row 12: K6 [5: 6: 6], P2, K2, P4, K6 [7: 7: 8], P2, K5, P2, K6 [7: 7: 8], P4, K2, P2, K6 [5: 6: 6].

Row 13: (Inc purlwise into first st) 0 [1: 1: 1] times, P6 [4: 5: 5], Cr3L, Cr3R, Cr3L, P5 [6: 6: 7], Cr3L, P3, Cr3R, P5 [6: 6: 7], Cr3R, Cr3L, Cr3R, P6 [4: 5: 5], (inc purlwise into last st) 0 [1: 1: 1] times. 49 [51: 53: 55] sts.

Row 14: K7 [7: 8: 8], P4, K2, P2, K6 [7: 7: 8], P2, K3, P2, K6 [7: 7: 8], P2, K2, P4, K7 [7: 8: 8].

Row 15: P7 [7: 8: 8], C4B, P2, K2, P6 [7: 7: 8], Cr3L, P1, Cr3R, P6 [7: 7: 8], K2, P2, C4F, P7 [7: 8: 8].

Row 16: K7 [7: 8: 8], P4, K2, P2, K7 [8: 8: 9], P2, K1, P2, K7 [8: 8: 9], P2, K2, P4, K7 [7: 8: 8].

These 16 rows form patt.

Keeping patt correct as now set, inc 1 st at each end of next [next: next: 3rd] and every foll 6th [4th: 4th: 6th] row until there are 53 [57: 57: 67] sts, then on every foll - [6th: 6th: -] row until there are - [59: 63: -] sts.

Cont straight until Sleeve meas 15 [17: 20: 24] cm (6 [6¾: 8: 9½] in), ending with RS facing for next row.

Shape Top

Keeping patt correct, cast off 5 [6: 4: 5] sts at beg of next 2 [4: 4: 12] rows, then 6 [7: 5: 0] sts at beg of foll 6 [4: 8: 0] rows.

Cast off rem 7 sts.

RIGHT SLEEVE

Work as given for Left Sleeve changing the **Cr5R** on row 1 of the 16 row patt rep to **Cr5L** throughout sleeve.

MAKING UP

Button Band

With RS facing, using 3.25 mm (US 3) needles cast on 1 st (this st will be used for sewing the band to left front opening edge), patt across 6 sts from Button Band holder. 7 sts.

Cont working in double moss st as set until band is of sufficient length to go up left front opening edge to start of neck shaping when slightly stretched, ending with RS facing for next row.

Cast off in patt.

Mark positions for 5 [5: 6: 6] buttons - the first to correspond with buttonhole on Right Front band, the last to be 1 cm (½ in) from cast-off edge and rem 3 [3: 4: 4] to be spaced evenly between. Slip stitch Button Band to opening front edge.

Buttonhole Band

With **WS** facing, using 3.25 mm (US 3) needles cast on 1 st (this st will be used for sewing the band to right front opening edge), patt across 6 sts from Buttonhole Band holder. 7 sts.

Cont working in double moss st as set until band is of sufficient length to go up right front opening edge to start of neck shaping when slightly stretched, ending with RS facing for next row, working buttonholes to correspond with markers as folls:

Next row (RS): Patt 3 sts, cast off next 2 sts, patt 1.

Next row: Patt 2, cast on 2 sts, patt 3.

Cast off in patt. Slip stitch Buttonhole Band to opening front edge.

Collar

Join shoulder seams.

With RS facing, using 3.25 mm (US 3) needles and starting halfway across buttonhole border, pick up and knit 15 [15: 16: 17] sts up right side of front neck, K across 18 [20: 22: 22] sts on back holder, then pick up and knit 15 [15: 16: 17] sts down left side of front neck ending half way across button band. 48 [50: 54: 56] sts.

Next row (RS): K15 [14: 16: 17], (inc knitwise into next st, K1) 9 [11: 11: 11] times, K15 [14: 16: 17]. 57 [61: 65: 67] sts.

Work 16 rows in double moss st as given for Back, ending with **WS** facing for next row.

Cast off **loosely** in patt.

Mark points along side seam edges 11 [12: 13: 14] cm (4¼ [4¾: 5: 5½] in) either side of shoulder seams, then sew shaped cast-off edge of sleeve to back and front between these points, taking care to sew the right and left sleeves to the correct side. Join side and sleeve seams. Sew on buttons.

Pin out garment to measurements given, cover with damp cloths and leave to dry naturally. See ball band for washing and further care instructions.

SKILL LEVEL

CARLO

SIZE

AGE	0-6 months	6-12 months	1-2 years	2-3 years
To fit chest				
	41	46	51	56 cm
	16	18	20	22 in
Actual chest measurement				
	45	51	55	60 cm
	17¾	20	21¾	23¾ in
Full length, from back neck				
	24	28	32	38 cm
	9½	11	12½	15 in
Sleeve length				
	15	17	20	24 cm
	6	6½	8	9½ in

YARN

Jody Long Ciao

4 [4: 5: 6] x 50g balls in Marigold 015

NEEDLES

1 pair 3.25 mm (no 10) (US 3) needles
1 pair 4 mm (no 8) (US 6) needles
Cable needle

TENSION

22 sts and 30 rows to 10 cm (4 in) measured over reversed st st, 26 sts and 34 rows to 10 cm (4 in) measured over honeycomb cable, both using 4 mm (US 6) needles.

ABBREVIATIONS

See inside front flap

SPECIAL ABBREVIATIONS

Cr3L = slip next 2 sts onto cable needle and leave at front of work, P1, then K2 from cable needle.
Cr3R = slip next st onto cable needle and leave at back of work, K2, then P1 from cable needle.
C4B = slip next 2 sts onto a cable needle and leave at back of work, K2, then K2 from cable needle.
C4F = slip next 2 sts onto a cable needle and leave at front of work, K2, then K2 from cable needle.

BACK

Using 3.25 mm (US 3) needles cast on 57 [63: 69: 75] sts.
Row 1 (RS): K3, *P3, K3, rep from * to end.
Row 2: P3, *K3, P3, rep from * to end.
These 2 rows for rib.
Work a further 7 [7: 9: 9] rows in rib, ending with **WS** facing for next row.
Next row (WS): P8 [9: 15: 17], inc **purlwise** into next st, (P9 [10: 18: 19], inc **purlwise** into next st), 4 [4: 2: 2] times, P8 [9: 15: 17]. 62 [68: 72: 78] sts.
Change to 4 mm (US 6) needles.
Now work in patt as folls:
Row 1 (RS): P5 [6: 6: 7], C4B, P4 [5: 6: 7], C4B, P2 [3: 4: 5], (C4B, C4F) 3 times, P2 [3: 4: 5], C4F, P4 [5: 6: 7], C4F, P5 [6: 6: 7].
Row 2: K5 [6: 6: 7], P4, K4 [5: 6: 7], P4, K2 [3: 4: 5], P24, K2 [3: 4: 5], P4, K4 [5: 6: 7], P4, K5 [6: 6: 7].
Row 3: P4 [5: 5: 6], Cr3R, Cr3L, P3 [4: 5: 6], K4, P2 [3: 4: 5], K24, P2 [3: 4: 5], K4, P3 [4: 5: 6], Cr3R, Cr3L, P4 [5: 5: 6].
Row 4: K4 [5: 5: 6], P2, K2, P2, K3 [4: 5: 6], P4, K2 [3: 4: 5], P24, K2 [3: 4: 5], P4, K3 [4: 5: 6], P2, K2, P2, K4 [5: 5: 6].
Row 5: P3 [4: 4: 5], Cr3R, P2, Cr3L, P2 [3: 4: 5], C4B, P2 [3: 4: 5],

(C4F, C4B) 3 times, P2 [3: 4: 5], C4F, P2 [3: 4: 5], Cr3R, P2, Cr3L, P3 [4: 4: 5].

Row 6: K3 [4: 4: 5], P2, K4, P2, K2 [3: 4: 5], P4, K2 [3: 4: 5], P24, K2 [3: 4: 5], P4, K2 [3: 4: 5], P2, K4, P2, K3 [4: 4: 5].

Row 7: P3 [4: 4: 5], K2, P4, K2, P2 [3: 4: 5], K4, P2 [3: 4: 5], K24, P2 [3: 4: 5], K4, P2 [3: 4: 5], K2, P4, K2, P3 [4: 4: 5].

Row 8: As row 6.

Row 9: P3 [4: 4: 5], Cr3L, P2, Cr3R, P2 [3: 4: 5], C4B, P2 [3: 4: 5], (C4B, C4F) 3 times, P2 [3: 4: 5], C4F, P2 [3: 4: 5], Cr3L, P2, Cr3R, P3 [4: 4: 5].

Row 10: As row 4.

Row 11: P4 [5: 5: 6], Cr3L, Cr3R, P3 [4: 5: 6], K4, P2 [3: 4: 5], K24, P2 [3: 4: 5], K4, P3 [4: 5: 6], Cr3L, Cr3R, P4 [5: 5: 6].

Row 12: As row 2.

Row 13: P5 [6: 6: 7], C4B, P4 [5: 6: 7], C4B, P2 [3: 4: 5], (C4F, C4B) 3 times, P2 [3: 4: 5], C4F, P4 [5: 6: 7], C4F, P5 [6: 6: 7].

Row 14: As row 2.

Row 15: P5 [6: 6: 7], K4, P4 [5: 6: 7], K4, P2 [3: 4: 5], K24, P2 [3: 4: 5], K4, P4 [5: 6: 7], K4, P5 [6: 6: 7].

Row 16: As row 2.

These 16 rows form patt.

Cont in patt until Back meas 24 [28: 32: 38] cm (9½ [11: 12½: 15] in), ending with RS facing for next row.

Shape Shoulders

Keeping patt correct, cast off 9 [10: 11: 12] sts at beg of next 2 rows, then 10 [11: 11: 13] sts at beg of foll 2 rows.

Cast off rem 24 [26: 28: 28] sts.

FRONT

Work as given for Back until 24 [26: 28: 30] rows less have been worked than on Back to beg of shoulder shaping, ending with RS facing for next row.

Shape Front Neck

Next row (RS): Patt 19 [21: 22: 25] and turn, leaving rem sts on a holder.

Cont working on these 19 [21: 22: 25] sts only as folls:

Work 23 [25: 27: 29] rows, ending with RS facing for next row.

Shape Shoulder

Keeping patt correct, cast off 9 [10: 11: 12] sts at beg of next row.

Work 1 row.

Cast off rem 10 [11: 11: 13] sts.

With RS facing, return to sts on holder, rejoin yarn and cast off central 24 [26: 28: 28] sts, patt to end. 19 [21: 22: 25] sts.

Cont working on these 19 [21: 22: 25] sts only as folls:

Work 23 [25: 27: 29] rows, ending with RS facing for next row.

Shape Shoulder

Work 1 row.

Keeping patt correct, cast off 9 [10: 11: 12] sts at beg of next row.

Work 1 row.

Cast off rem 10 [11: 11: 13] sts.

SLEEVES
LEFT SLEEVE

Using 3.25 mm (US 3) needles cast on 39 [39: 39: 45] sts.

Row 1 (RS): K3, *P3, K3, rep from * to end.

Row 2: P3, *K3, P3, rep from * to end.

These 2 rows for rib.

Work a further 7 [7: 9: 9] rows in rib, ending with **WS** facing for next row.

0-6 Months, 6-12 Months and 1-2 Years Only

Next row (WS): Purl inc 1 [1: 3] sts evenly across row. 40 [40: 42] sts.

2-3 Years Only

Next row (WS): Purl dec 1 st at centre of row. [44] sts.

All Sizes

Change to 4 mm (US 6) needles. **

Now work in patt as folls:

Row 1 (RS): P10 [9: 9: 9], (C4B, P4 [5: 6: 7]) twice, C4F, P10 [9: 9: 9].

Row 2: K10 [9: 9: 9], (P4, K4 [5: 6: 7]) twice, P4, K10 [9: 9: 9].

Row 3: P10 [9: 9: 9], K4, P3 [4: 5: 6], Cr3R, Cr3L, P3 [4: 5: 6], K4, P10 [9: 9: 9].

Row 4: K10 [9: 9: 9], P4, K3 [4: 5: 6], P2, K2, P2, K3 [4: 5: 6], P4, K10 [9: 9: 9].

Row 5: (Inc **purlwise** into first st) 0 [1: 1: 1] times, P10 [8: 8: 8], C4B, P2 [3: 4: 5], Cr3R, P2, Cr3L, P2 [3: 4: 5], C4F, P10 [8: 8: 8], (inc **purlwise** into last st) 0 [1: 1: 1] times. 40 [42: 44: 46] sts.

Row 6: K10, P4, K2 [3: 4: 5], P2, K4, P2, K2 [3: 4: 5], P4, K10.

Row 7: P10, K4, P2 [3: 4: 5], K2, P4, K2, P2 [3: 4: 5], K4, P10.

Row 8: As row 6.

Row 9: P10, C4B, P2 [3: 4: 5], Cr3L, P2, Cr3R, P2 [3: 4: 5], C4F, P10.

Row 10: K10, P4, K3 [4: 5: 6], P2, K2, P2, K3 [4: 5: 6], P4, K10.

Row 11: (Inc **purlwise** into first st) 1 [0: 1: 1] times, P9 [10: 9: 9], K4, P3 [4: 5: 6], Cr3L, Cr3R, P3 [4: 5: 6], K4, P9 [10: 9: 9], (inc **purlwise** into last st) 1 [0: 1: 1] times. 42 [42: 46: 48] sts.

Row 12: K11 [10: 11: 11], (P4, K4 [5: 6: 7]) twice, P4, K11 [10: 11: 11].

Row 13: (Inc **purlwise** into first st) 0 [1: 0: 0] times, P11 [9: 11: 11], (C4B, P4 [5: 6: 7]) twice, C4F, P11 [9: 11: 11], (inc **purlwise** into last st) 0 [1: 0: 0] times. 42 [44: 46: 48] sts.

Row 14: K11, (P4, K4 [5: 6: 7]) twice, P4, K11.

Row 15: P11, (K4, P4 [5: 6: 7]) twice, K4, P11.

Row 16: As row 14.

These 16 rows set patt and start sleeve shaping.

***Cont as set, inc 1 st at each end of 7th [5th: 3rd: next] and 0 [1: 2: 1] foll - [8th: 8th: 6th] row, then on 0 [0: 0: 3] foll - [-: -: 8th] row, taking inc sts into reverse st st. 44 [48: 52: 58] sts.

Cont straight until Sleeve meas 15 [17: 20: 24] cm (6 [6½: 8: 9½] in), ending with RS facing for next row.

Shape Top

Keeping patt correct, cast off 3 sts at beg of next 12 [8: 12: 14] rows, then 0 [4: 4: 4] sts at beg of foll 0 [4: 2: 2] rows.

Cast off rem 8 sts.

RIGHT SLEEVE

Work as given for Left Sleeve to **.

Now work in patt as folls:

Row 1 (RS): P10 [9: 9: 9], C4B, (P4 [5: 6: 7], C4F) twice, P10 [9: 9: 9].

Row 2: K10 [9: 9: 9], (P4, K4 [5: 6: 7]) twice, P4, K10 [9: 9: 9].

Row 3: P10 [9: 9: 9], K4, P3 [4: 5: 6], Cr3R, Cr3L, P3 [4: 5: 6], K4, P10 [9: 9: 9].

Row 4: K10 [9: 9: 9], P4, K3 [4: 5: 6], P2, K2, P2, K3 [4: 5: 6], P4, K10 [9: 9: 9].

Row 5: (Inc **purlwise** into first st) 0 [1: 1: 1] times, P10 [8: 8: 8], C4B, P2 [3: 4: 5], Cr3R, P2, Cr3L, P2 [3: 4: 5], C4F, P10 [8: 8: 8], (inc **purlwise** into last st) 0 [1: 1: 1] times. 40 [42: 44: 46] sts.

Row 6: K10, P4, K2 [3: 4: 5], P2, K4, P2, K2 [3: 4: 5], P4, K10.

Row 7: P10, K4, P2 [3: 4: 5], K2, P4, K2, P2 [3: 4: 5], K4, P10.

Row 8: As row 6.

Row 9: P10, C4B, P2 [3: 4: 5], Cr3L, P2, Cr3R, P2 [3: 4: 5], C4F, P10.

Row 10: K10, P4, K3 [4: 5: 6], P2, K2, P2, K3 [4: 5: 6], P4, K10.

Row 11: (Inc **purlwise** into first st) 1 [0: 1: 1] times, P9 [10: 9: 9], K4, P3 [4: 5: 6], Cr3L, Cr3R, P3 [4: 5: 6], K4, P9 [10: 9: 9], (inc **purlwise** into last st) 1 [0: 1: 1] times. 42 [42: 46: 48] sts.

Row 12: K11 [10: 11: 11], (P4, K4 [5: 6: 7]) twice, P4, K11 [10: 11: 11].

Row 13: (Inc **purlwise** into first st) 0 [1: 0: 0] times, P11 [9: 11: 11], C4B, (P4 [5: 6: 7], C4F) twice, P11 [9: 11: 11], (inc **purlwise** into last st) 0 [1: 0: 0] times. 42 [44: 46: 48] sts.

Row 14: K11, (P4, K4 [5: 6: 7]) twice, P4, K11.

Row 15: P11, (K4, P4 [5: 6: 7]) twice, K4, P11.

Row 16: As row 14.

These 16 rows set patt and start sleeve shaping.

Now work as given for Left Sleeve from *** to end.

MAKING UP

Collar

Using 3.25 mm (US 3) needles cast on 124 [124: 136: 136] sts.

Row 1 (WS): K1, (P3, K3) 4 [4: 5: 5] times, (P4, K3) 10 times, P4, (K3, P3) 4 [4: 5: 5] times, K1.

Row 2: K1, (K3, P3) 4 [4: 5: 5] times, (K4, P3) 10 times, K4, (P3, K3) 4 [4: 5: 5] times, K1.

Rows 3 and 4: As rows 1 and 2.

Row 5: As row 1.

Row 6: K1, (K3, P3) 4 [4: 5: 5] times, (K1, K2tog, K1, P3) 10 times, K1, K2tog, K1, (P3, K3) 4 [4: 5: 5] times, K1. 113 [113: 125: 125] sts.

Now work in rib as folls:

Row 1 (WS): K1, P3, *K3, P3, rep from * to last st, K1.

Row 2: K1, *K3, P3, rep from * to last 4 sts, K4.

Last 2 rows form rib.

Cont in rib until Collar meas 8 [9: 10: 12] cm (3 [3½: 4: 4¾] in), ending with **WS** facing for next row.

Cast off **loosely** in rib (on **WS**).

Join shoulder seams. Mark points along side seam edges 10 [11: 12: 13] cm (4 [4¼: 4¾: 5] in) either side of shoulder seams, then sew shaped cast-off edge of sleeve to back and front between these points points, taking care to sew the right and left sleeves to the correct side. Join side and sleeve seams. Placing left side of collar over right side, sew edges of collar to cast-off sts at front of neck. Sew cast-off edges of collar evenly in position all around neck edge.

Pin out garment to measurements given, cover with damp cloths and leave to dry naturally. See ball band for washing and further care instructions.

SKILL LEVEL

DARIO HAT

SIZES

AGE	0-6 months	6-12 months	1-2 years	2-3 years
Circumference around head				
	33.5	36.5	39	43.5 cm
	13¼	14½	15½	17¼ in

YARN

Jody Long Ciao
For Striped Version
A 1 [1: 1: 1] x 50g balls in Lead 003
B 1 [1: 1: 1] x 50g balls in Chrome 004
For Plain Version
1 [1: 2: 2] x 50g balls in Marine 008

NEEDLES

1 pair 3.25 mm (no 10) (US 3) needles
1 pair 4 mm (no 8) (US 6) needles

BUTTONS - 1 [1: 1: 1]

TENSION

22 sts and 30 rows to 10 cm (4 in) measured over st st using 4 mm (US 6) needles.

ABBREVIATIONS

See inside front flap

STRIPED HELMET
LEFT EAR FLAP

Using 3.25 mm (US 3) needles and yarn **A** cast on 5 sts.
Work in g st throughout and noting that first row is RS, work as folls:
Work 5 rows, ending with **WS** facing for next row.
Next row (WS): K2, yo, K2tog (to make a buttonhole), K1.
Work 6 rows, ending with RS facing for next row.
Next row (RS): K1, M1, K to last st, M1, K1. 7 sts.
Work 1 row.
Next row (RS): K1, M1, K to last st, M1, K1. 9 sts.
Work 3 rows.
Next row (RS): K1, M1, K to last st, M1, K1.
Rep the last 4 rows once more, ending with **WS** facing for next row. 13 sts. Place a marker at centre of last row.
Cont in g st without shaping until ear flap meas 2 [3: 3: 4] cm (¾ [1¼: 1¼: 1½] in), **from marker**, ending with RS facing for next row.
Break off yarn and slip these 13 sts onto a holder.

RIGHT EAR FLAP

Work as given for the Left Ear Flap omitting buttonhole.

MAIN SECTION

Using 3.25 mm (US 3) needles and yarn **A** cast on 10 [12: 14: 18] sts, with RS of work facing knit across 13 sts of Left Ear Flap, cast on 28 [30: 32: 34] sts, with RS facing knit across 13 sts of Right Ear

Flap, cast on 10 [12: 14: 18] sts. 74 [80: 86: 96] sts.
Next row (WS): Knit.
Cont in g st until the Main Section of the Helmet meas 5 [5: 6: 6] cm (2 [2: 2½: 2½] in), ending with RS facing for next row.
Change to 4 mm (US 6) needles.
Beg with a K row, work in striped st st for the remainder of the Helmet by alternating 2 rows using yarn **B** and 2 rows using yarn **A** throughout.
Work straight until the Main Section meas 11 [12: 13: 14] cm (4¼ [4¾: 5¼: 5½] in), ending with **WS** facing for next row.

0-6 Months and 2-3 Years Only
Next row (WS): Purl, inc 4 [-: -: 3] sts evenly across the row. 78 [-: -: 99] sts.

6-12 Months and 1-2 Years Only
Next row (WS): Purl, dec - [2: 1: -] sts evenly across the row. - [78: 85: -] sts.

For All Sizes
Shape Crown
Keeping stripes correct throughout, work as folls:
Row 1 (RS): K1, (K2tog, K5) 11 [11: 12: 14] times. 67 [67: 73: 85] sts.
Beg with a P row, work 3 rows in st st, ending with RS facing for next row.
Row 5 (RS): K1, (K2tog, K4) 11 [11:12: 14] times. 56 [56: 61: 71] sts.
Row 6 and every foll alt row: Purl.
Row 7: K1, (K2tog, K3) 11 [11: 12: 14] times. 45 [45: 49: 57] sts.
Row 9: K1, (K2tog, K2) 11 [11: 12: 14] times. 34 [34: 37: 43] sts.
Row 11: K1, (K2tog, K1) 11 [11: 12: 14] times. 23 [23: 25: 29] sts.
Row 13: K1, (K2tog) 11 [11: 12: 14] times. 12 [12: 13: 15] sts.
Break off yarn, thread through rem 12 [12: 13: 15] sts, pull up tightly and fasten off.

MAKING UP

Join back seam by joining row-ends together.
Cover with damp cloths and leave to dry naturally. See ball band for washing and further care instructions.

PLAIN HELMET

Work as given for striped version, but using one colour throughout.

DINO HAT

SIZES

AGE	0-6 months	6-12 months	1-2 years	2-3 years
Measurement around lower edge				
	34	36	38	41 cm
	13½	14¼	15	16 in

YARN
Jody Long Ciao
A 1 [1: 2: 2] x 50g balls in Cocoa 005
B 1 [1: 1: 1] x 50g balls in Marigold 015

NEEDLES
1 pair 3.25 mm (no 10) (US 3) needles
1 pair 4 mm (no 8) (US 6) needles

TENSION
22 sts and 30 rows to 10 cm (4 in) measured over st st using 4 mm (US 6) needles.

ABBREVIATIONS
See inside front flap

HAT
Using 3.25 mm (US 3) needles and yarn **B** cast on 90 [94: 98: 106] sts.
Row 1 (RS): K2, *P2, K2, rep from * to end.
Break off yarn **B** and join in yarn **A**.
Continue in yarn **A** for the remainder of Hat as folls:
Row 2 (WS): P2, *K2, P2, rep from * to end.
Row 3: K2, *P2, K2, rep from * to end.
These 2 rows form rib.
Cont in rib for a further 4 [4: 6: 6] rows, ending with **WS** facing for next row.

Next row (WS): P2 [4: 6: 3], P2tog, (P4 [4: 4: 5], P2tog) 14 times, P2 [4: 6: 3]. 75 [79: 83: 91] sts.
Change to 4 mm (US 6) needles.
Beg with a K row, work in st st until Hat meas 18 [19: 20: 21] cm (7 [7½: 8: 8¼] in), ending with **WS** [RS: **WS**: RS] facing for next row.

0-6 Months Only
Next row (WS): P18, P2tog, P36, P2tog, P18. 73 sts.

1-2 Years Only
Next row (WS): P21, M1P, P41, M1P, P21. [85] sts.

All Sizes
Shape Crown
Row 1 (RS): K1, *K2tog, K4, rep from * to end. 61 [66: 71: 76] sts.
Work 3 rows, ending with RS facing for next row.
Row 5: K1, *K2tog, K3, rep from * to end. 49 [53: 57: 61] sts.
Row 6 and every foll alt row: Purl.
Row 7: K1, *K2tog, K2, rep from * to end. 37 [40: 43: 46] sts.
Row 9: K1, *K2tog, K1, rep from * to end. 25 [27: 29: 31] sts.
Row 11: K1, (K2tog) to end. 13 [14: 15: 16] sts.
Row 12: (P2tog) 6 [7: 7: 8] times, P1 [0: 1: 0].
Break off yarn and thread through rem 7 [7: 8: 8] sts, pull up tightly and fasten off securely.

MAKING UP
Join centre back seam by joining row-ends together.
Cover with damp cloths and leave to dry naturally. See ball band for washing and further care instructions.

DONATELLA

SIZE

AGE	0-6 months	6-12 months	1-2 years	2-3 years
To fit chest				
	41	46	51	56 cm
	16	18	20	22 in
Actual chest measurement				
	47.5	52.5	57	61.5 cm
	18¾	20¾	22½	24¼ in
Full length, from shoulder				
	24	28	32	38 cm
	9½	11	12½	15 in
Sleeve length				
	15	17	20	24 cm
	6	6½	8	9½ in

YARN

Jody Long Ciao
A 3 [4: 4: 5] x 50g balls in Fuchsia 019
B 1 [1: 1: 1] x 50g balls in Marigold 015
C 1 [1: 1: 1] x 50g balls in Avocado 011

NEEDLES

1 pair 3.25 mm (no 10) (US 3) needles
1 pair 4 mm (no 8) (US 6) needles

BUTTONS - 5 [5: 6: 6]

TENSION

22 sts and 37 rows to 10 cm (4 in) measured over moss st using 4 mm (US 6) needles.

ABBREVIATIONS

See inside front flap

BODY (Worked in one piece to armholes)

Using 4 mm (US 6) needles and yarn **B** cast on 105 [115: 125: 135] sts.
Row 1 (RS): K1, *P1, K1, rep from * to end.
Row 2: As row 1.
These 2 rows form moss st.
Joining in and breaking off colours as required, cont in moss st throughout as folls:
Rows 3 to 6: Using yarn **A**.
Rows 7 and 8: Using yarn **B**.
Rows 9 and 10: Using yarn **A**.
Rows 11 and 12: Using yarn **B**.
Rows 13 to 16: Using yarn **A**.
Rows 17 and 18: Using yarn **B**.
Rows 19 and 20: Using yarn **A**.
Rows 21 and 22: Using yarn **B**.
Break off yarn **B** and cont in yarn **A** only as folls:
Cont in moss st until Body meas 14 [17: 20: 25] cm (5½ [6½: 8: 9¾] in), ending with RS facing for next row.

Divide For Armholes

Next row (RS): Patt 25 [27: 29: 31] sts and slip these sts onto a holder (for right front), patt 55 [61: 67: 73] sts and turn, leaving rem 25: 27: 29: 31] sts on another holder (for left front).
Keeping moss st correct, work on this set of 55 [61: 67: 73] sts only for Back section as folls:
Work 1 row, ending with RS facing for next row.
Dec 1 st at each end of next 7 [7: 9: 9] rows, then on 2 [3: 2: 3] foll alt rows. 37 [41: 45: 49] sts.
Cont straight until armhole meas 10 [11: 12: 13] cm (4 [4¼: 4¾: 5] in), ending with RS facing for next row.

Shape Shoulders

Keeping patt correct, cast off 4 [5: 5: 6] sts at beg of next 2 rows, then 5 [5: 6: 6] sts at beg of foll 2 rows.

Break yarn and leave rem 19 [21: 23: 25] sts on a holder for Neckband).

Shape Left Front

Slip 25 [27: 29: 31] sts on left front holder onto 4 mm (US 6) needles and rejoin yarn **A** with RS facing.

Keeping moss st correct, cont as folls:

Work 2 rows, ending with RS facing for next row.

Dec 1 st at armhole edge of next 7 [7: 9: 9] rows, then on 2 [3: 2: 3] foll alt rows. 16 [17: 18: 19] sts.

Cont straight until 16 [16: 18: 18] rows less have been worked than on Back to beg of shoulder shaping, ending with RS facing for next row.

Shape Front Neck

Next row (RS): Patt 14 [15: 16: 17] sts, and turn, leaving rem 2 sts on a holder (for Neckband).

Keeping patt correct, dec 1 st at neck edge of next 2 rows, then on foll alt row, then on 2 foll 4th rows. 9 [10: 11: 12] sts.

Work 3 [3: 5: 5] rows, ending with RS facing for next row.

Shape Shoulder

Keeping patt correct, cast off 4 [5: 5: 6] sts at beg of next row.

Work 1 row.

Cast off rem 5 [5: 6: 6] sts.

Shape Right Front

Slip 25 [27: 29: 31] sts on right front holder onto 4 mm (US 6) needles and rejoin yarn **A** with **WS** facing.

Keeping moss st correct, cont as folls:

Work 1 row, ending with RS facing for next row.

Dec 1 st at armhole edge of next 7 [7: 9: 9] rows, then on 2 [3: 2: 3] foll alt rows. 16 [17: 18: 17] sts.

Cont straight until 16 [16: 18: 18] rows less have been worked than on Back to beg of shoulder shaping, ending with RS facing for next row.

Shape Front Neck

Next row (RS): Slip first 2 sts onto a holder (for Neckband), rejoin yarn **A** to rem sts, patt to end. 14 [15: 16: 17] sts.

Keeping patt correct, dec 1 st at neck edge of next 2 rows, then on foll alt row, then on 2 foll 4th rows. 9 [10: 11: 12] sts.

Work 4 [4: 6: 6] rows, ending with **WS** facing for next row.

Shape Shoulder

Keeping patt correct, cast off 4 [5: 5: 6] sts at beg of next row.

Work 1 row.

Cast off rem 5 [5: 6: 6] sts.

SLEEVES

Using 4 mm (US 6) needles and yarn **B** cast on 27: 29: 31: 33] sts.

Row 1 (RS): K1, *P1, K1, rep from * to end.

Row 2: As row 1.

These 2 rows form moss st.

Joining in and breaking off colours as required, cont in moss stitch throughout as folls:

Rows 3 to 6: Using yarn **A**.

Rows 7 and 8: Using yarn **B**.

Rows 9 and 10: Using yarn **A**.

Rows 11 and 12: Using yarn **B**.

Break off yarn **B** and cont in yarn **A** only as folls:

Cont in moss st work as folls:

Inc 1 st at each end of next [next: 3rd: 3rd] and every foll 4th [4th: 4th: 6th] row until there are 35 [35: 35: 49] sts, then on 3 [5: 7: 3] foll 6th [6th: 6th: 8th] rows, taking inc sts into moss st. 43 [47: 51: 55] sts.

Cont straight until Sleeve meas 15 [17: 20: 24] cm (6 [6¾: 8: 9½] in), ending with RS facing for next row.

Shape Top

Place markers at both ends of last row (to denote top of sleeve seam).

Keeping patt correct, dec 1 st at each end of next 7 [7: 9: 9] rows, then on 2 [3: 2: 3] foll alt rows, then on foll row, ending with RS facing for next row. 25 [27: 29: 31] sts.

Cast off in moss st.

ROSES (Make 3)

Using 3.25 mm (US 3) needles and yarn **B** cast on 27 [29: 31: 33] sts.

Beg with a K row, work in st st for 3 rows, ending with **WS** facing for next row.

Next row (WS): K1, *yo, K2tog, rep from * to end.

Beg with a K row, work in st st for 3 rows, ending with **WS** facing for next row.

Cast off **purlwise** (on **WS**).

LEAVES (Make 3)

Using 3.25 mm (US 3) needles and yarn **C** cast on 11 [11: 13: 13] sts.

Now work as folls:

Rows 1 and 2: K9 [9: 11: 11], turn and K to end.

Rows 3 and 4: K7 [7: 9: 9], turn and K to end.

Rows 5 and 6: K4 [4: 6: 6], turn and K to end.

Row 7 (RS): Knit across **all** 11 [11: 13: 13] sts.

Cast off **knitwise** (on **WS**).

MAKING UP

Join both shoulder seams.

Button Band

Using 3.25 mm (US 3) needles and yarn **A** cast on 1 st (this first st will be used for sewing the border to left front opening edge), cast on a further 5 sts. 6 sts.

Work entirely in g st until the button band is long enough to reach the start of neck shaping when slightly stretched, ending with RS facing for next row.

Slip these 6 sts onto a holder (for Neckband).

Mark positions for 5 [5: 6: 6] buttons the first one to be on 5th row from lower edge and the last one will be worked on first row of Neckband, the rem 3 [3: 4: 4] evenly spaced between these two.

Buttonhole Band

Using 3.25 mm (US 3) needles and yarn **A** cast on 5 sts, cast on a further 1 st (this last st will be used for sewing the border to right

front opening edge). 6 sts.
Work entirely in g st, work as folls:
Work 4 rows, ending with RS facing for next row.

Buttonhole Row (RS): K2, yo, K2tog (to make a buttonhole), K2.
Now cont in g st until the buttonhole band is long enough to reach the start of neck shaping when slightly stretched, ending with RS facing for next row and working buttonholes on RS rows like before to correspond with markers on Button Band.
Do not break yarn.

Neckband

With RS facing, using 3.25 mm (US 3) needles and yarn **A**, work across the 6 sts of buttonhole band as folls: K2, yo, K2tog (to make 5th [5th: 6th: 6th] buttonhole), K2tog, K across 2 sts on right front holder, pick up and knit 16 [17: 18: 19] sts up right side of front neck, K across 19 [21: 23: 25] sts on back holder, pick up and knit 16 [17: 18: 19] sts down left side of front neck, then K across 2 sts on left front holder, then work across the 6 sts of button band as folls: K2tog, K4. 65 [69: 73: 77] sts.

Work in g st for 4 rows, ending with WS facing for next row.
Cast off **knitwise** (on **WS**).

Join sleeve seams. Sew sleeves into armholes. Slip stitch front bands to corresponding front opening edge. Sew on buttons.
With RS outside fold each Rose piece in half so that cast-on and cast-off edges meet and oversew edges together. Tightly roll up doubled strip to form a rose shape as in photograph and sew through base to secure. Using photograph as a guide sew 3 Roses onto Right Front to form a cluster. Attach a leaf between each of the 3 Roses as in photograph.

Pin out garment to measurements given and cover with damp cloths, and leave to dry naturally, taking care not to flatten the Roses. See ball band for washing and further care instructions.

FABIANA HAT

SIZES

AGE	0-6 months	6-12 months	1-2 years	2-3 years
Measurement around lower edge				
	32	35	38.5	42 cm
	12½	13¾	15¼	16½ in

YARN

Jody Long Ciao

A 1 [1: 1: 2] x 50g balls in Fuchsia 019
B 1 [1: 1: 1] x 50g balls in Marigold 015
C 1 [1: 1: 1] x 50g balls in Avocado 011

NEEDLES

1 pair 3.25 mm (no 10) (US 3) needles
1 pair 4 mm (no 8) (US 6) needles

TENSION

22 sts and 37 rows to 10 cm (4 in) measured over moss st using 4 mm (US 6) needles.

ABBREVIATIONS

See inside front flap

HAT

Using 4 mm (US 6) needles and yarn **B** cast on 71 [77: 85: 93] sts.
Row 1 (RS): K1, *P1, K1, rep from * to end.
Row 2: As row 1.
These 2 rows form moss st.
Joining in and breaking off colours as required, cont in moss stitch throughout as folls:
Rows 3 to 6: Using yarn **A**.
Rows 7 and 8: Using yarn **B**.
Rows 9 and 10: Using yarn **A**.
Rows 11 and 12: Using yarn **B**.
Break off yarn **B** and cont in yarn **A** only as folls:
Cont in moss st until Hat meas 10 [11: 12: 13] cm (4 [4¼: 4¾: 5¼] in), ending with RS facing for next row.

Shape Crown

Keeping moss stitch correct, work as folls:
Row 1 (RS): Patt 3, P3tog, *patt 7, P3tog, rep from * to last 5 [1: 9: 7] sts, patt 5 [1: 9: 7]. 57 [61: 69: 75] sts.
Work 5 rows, ending with RS facing for next row.
Row 7: Patt 3, P3tog, *patt 5, P3tog, rep from * to last 3 [7: 7: 5] sts, patt 3 [7: 7: 5]. 43 [47: 53: 57] sts.
Work 3 rows, ending with RS facing for next row.
Row 11: Patt 3, P3tog, *patt 3, P3tog, rep from * to last 1 [5: 5: 3] sts, patt 1 [5: 5: 3] sts. 29 [33: 37: 39] sts.
Work 3 rows, ending with RS facing for next row.
Row 15: Patt 3, P3tog, *K1, P3tog, rep from * to last 3 [3: 3: 1] sts, patt 3 [3: 3: 1]. 17 [19: 21: 21] sts.
Work 2 rows, ending with **WS** facing for next row.
Row 18 (WS): (P2tog) 8 [9: 10: 10] times, P1.
Break off yarn and thread through rem 9 [10: 11: 11] sts, pull up tightly and fasten off securely.

ROSES (Make 3)

Using 3.25 mm (US 3) needles and yarn **B** cast on 27 [29: 31: 33] sts.
Beg with a K row, work in st st for 3 rows, ending with **WS** facing for next row.
Next row (WS): K1, *yo, K2tog, rep from * to end.
Beg with a K row, work in st st for 3 rows, ending with **WS** facing for next row.
Cast off **purlwise** (on **WS**).

LEAVES (Make 3)

Using 3.25 mm (US 3) needles and yarn C cast on 11 [11: 13: 13] sts.
Now work as folls:
Rows 1 and 2: K9 [9: 11: 11], turn and K to end.
Rows 3 and 4: K7 [7: 9: 9], turn and K to end.
Rows 5 and 6: K4 [4: 6: 6], turn and K to end.
Row 7 (RS): Knit across **all** 11 [11: 13: 13] sts.
Cast off **knitwise** (on **WS**).

MAKING UP

Join centre back seam of Hat by joining row-ends together.
With RS outside fold each Rose piece in half so that cast-on and cast-off edges meet and oversew edges together. Tightly roll up doubled strip to form a rose shape as in photograph and sew through base to secure. Using photograph as a guide sew 3 Roses onto side of Hat to form a cluster. Attach a leaf between each of the 3 Roses as in photograph.
Cover with damp cloths and leave to dry naturally. See ball band for washing and further care instructions.

SKILL LEVEL

ENZO

SIZE

AGE	0-6 months	6-12 months	1-2 years	2-3 years
To fit chest				
	41	46	51	56 cm
	16	18	20	22 in
Actual chest measurement				
	45	51	56	62 cm
	17¾	20	22	24¼ in
Full length, from back neck				
	24	28	32	38 cm
	9½	11	12½	15 in
Sleeve length				
	15	17	20	24 cm
	6	6½	8	9½ in

YARN
Jody Long Ciao
A 1 [2: 2: 2] x 50g balls in Dijon 016
B 1 [2: 2: 2] x 50g balls in Lead 003
C 1 [1: 1: 1] x 50g ball in Marine 008
D 1 [1: 1: 1] x 50g ball in Alabaster 002

NEEDLES
1 pair 3.25 mm (no 10) (US 3) needles
1 pair 4 mm (no 8) (US 6) needles

BUTTONS - 3 [3: 3: 3]

TENSION
22 sts and 30 rows to 10 cm (4 in) measured over st st using 4 mm (US 6) needles.

ABBREVIATIONS
See inside front flap

BACK
Using 3.25 mm (US 3) needles and yarn **A** cast on 58 [66: 70: 78] sts.
Row 1 (RS): K2, *P2, K2, rep from * to end.
Row 2: P2, *K2, P2, rep from * to end.
These 2 rows form rib.
Work in rib for a further 7 [7: 11: 11] rows, ending with **WS** facing for next row.
Next row (WS): Rib 3 [5: 2: 2], work 2 tog, (rib 5 [4: 7: 6], work 2 tog) 7 [9: 7: 9] times, rib 4 [5: 3: 2]. 50 [56: 62: 68] sts.
Change to 4 mm (US 6) needles.
Beg with a K row, now work in st st throughout as folls: ******
Work 32 [40: 46: 62] rows, ending with RS facing for next row.
Break off yarn **A** and join in yarn **B**.
Work 2 rows, ending with RS facing for next row.

Shape Raglan Armholes
Cast off 3 sts at beg of next 2 rows. 44 [50: 56: 62] sts.
Dec 1 st at each end of next and 1 [1: 0: 0] foll 4th rows, then on foll 11 [13: 16: 18] alt rows. 18 [20: 22: 24] sts.
Work 1 row, ending with RS facing for next row.
Break yarn and leave sts on a holder (for Neckband).

POCKET LINING
Using 4 mm (US 6) needles and yarn **C** cast on 11 [12: 13: 14] sts.
Beg with a K row, now work in st st for 12 [14: 14: 16] rows, ending with RS facing for next row.
Break yarn and leave sts on a holder.

FRONT

Work as given for Back to **.

Work 31 [39: 45: 61] rows, ending with **WS** facing for next row.

Place Pocket

Next row (WS): P31 [35: 39: 43], cast off next 11 [12: 13: 14] sts **knitwise** (for pocket opening), P to end.

Break off yarn **A** and join in yarn **B**.

Next row (RS): K8 [9: 10: 11], K across 11 [12: 13: 14] sts of Pocket Lining, K to end. 50 [56: 62: 68] sts.

Work 1 row, ending with RS facing for next row.

Shape Raglan Armholes

Cast off 2 sts at beg of next row, then 3 sts at beg of foll row. 45 [51: 57: 63] sts.

Next row (RS): K4, P1, K2tog (for left raglan armhole decrease), K to last 2 sts, K2tog. 43 [49: 55: 61] sts.

Next row: P to last 5 sts, K1, P3, K1.

Last 2 rows set the sts – left raglan armhole edge 5 sts worked as buttonhole border with raglan dec worked next to these 5 sts, and right raglan armhole edge dec worked as for Back.

Keeping sts and raglan decreases correct as now set, work 0 [0: 2: 2] rows, dec 0 [0: 1: 1] st at both raglan edges of first of these rows. 43 [49: 53: 59] sts.

Next row (RS): K1, sl 1, K1, psso, yo (to make a buttonhole), K1, P1, (K2tog - for raglan dec) 0 [0: 1: 1] time, K to last 0 [0: 2: 2] sts, (K2tog) 0 [0: 1: 1] time. 43 [49: 51: 57] sts.

Working a 2nd buttonhole in same way as buttonhole just worked on foll 10th [12th: 12th: 14th] row and noting that no further reference will be made to buttonholes, cont as folls:

Dec 1 st at both raglan edges of 2nd and foll 6 [7: 6: 7] alt rows. 29 [33: 37: 41] sts.

Work 1 row, ending with RS facing for next row.

Shape Front Neck

Next row (RS): Patt 5 sts, K2tog, K3 [5: 7: 9] and turn, leaving rem sts on a holder.

Work on this set of 9 [11: 13: 15] sts only for first side of neck as folls:

0-6 Months Only

Next row (WS): P2tog, P2, K1, P3, K1. 8 sts.
Next row: K4, P1, K3tog. 6 sts.
Next row: P2tog, P3, K1. 5 sts.
Next row: K2, sl 1, K2tog, psso. 3 sts.
Next row: P2tog, K1. 2 sts.

6-12 Months Only

Next row (WS): P2tog, P4, K1, P3, K1. 10 sts.
Next row: K4, P1, K2tog, K1, K2tog. 8 sts.
Next row: P2tog, P1, K1, P3, K1. 7 sts.
Next row: K4, P3tog. 5 sts.
Next row: P2tog, P2, K1. 4 sts.
Next row: K1, sl 1, K2tog, psso. 2 sts.
Next row: P1, K1.

1-2 Years Only

Next row (WS): P2tog, P6, K1, P3, K1. 12 sts.

Next row: K4, P1, K2tog, K3, K2tog. 10 sts.
Next row: P2tog, (P3, K1) twice. 9 sts.
Next row: K4, P1, (K2tog) twice. 7 sts.
Next row: P2tog, K1, P3, K1. 6 sts.
Next row: K3, sl 1, K2tog, psso. 4 sts.
Next row: P3, K1.
Next row: K1, sl 1, K2tog, psso. 2 sts.
Next row: P1, K1.

2-3 Years Only

Next row (WS): P2tog, P8, K1, P3, K1. 14 sts.
Next row: K4, P1, K2tog, K5, K2tog. 12 sts.
Next row: P2tog, P5, K1, P3, K1. 11 sts.
Next row: K4, P1, K2tog, K2, K2tog. 9 sts.
Next row: P2tog, P2, K1, P3, K1. 8 sts.
Next row: K4, P1, K3tog. 6 sts.
Next row: P1, K1, P3, K1.
Next row: K3, sl 1, K2tog, psso. 4 sts.
Next row: P3, K1.
Next row: K1, sl 1, K2tog, psso. 2 sts.
Next row: P1, K1.

For All Sizes

Next row (RS): K2tog and fasten off.

Return to sts left on holder and slip centre 10 sts onto another holder (for Neckband). Rejoin yarn to rem sts with RS facing, K to last 2 sts, K2tog. 8 [10: 12: 14] sts.

Dec 1 st at neck edge of next 4 rows, then on foll 0 [1: 2: 3] alt rows **and at same time** dec 1 st at raglan armhole edge of 2nd and foll 1 [2: 3: 4] alt rows. 2 sts.

Work 1 row, ending with RS facing for next row.

Next row (RS): K2tog and fasten off.

LEFT SLEEVE

Using 3.25 mm (US 3) needles and yarn **C** cast on 26 [30: 30: 34] sts.

Work in rib as given for Back for 10 [10: 10: 12] rows, inc [dec: inc: dec] 1 st at centre of last row and ending with RS facing for next row. 27 [29: 31: 33] sts.

Change to 4 mm (US 6) needles.

Beg with a K row and joining in and breaking off colors as required, now work in st st throughout as folls:

0-6 Months and 2-3 Years Only

Work 2 rows, inc 1 st at each end of first of these rows. 29 [-: -: 35] sts.

All Sizes

Join in yarn **D**.

Using yarn **D**, work 4 [5: 6: 7] rows, inc 1 st at each end of next [next: next: 3rd] and 0 [1: 1: 1] foll 4th row. 31 [33: 35: 39] sts.

Using yarn **C**, work 4 [5: 6: 7] rows, inc 1 st at each end of next [4th: 3rd: 4th] row. 33 [35: 37: 41] sts.

Last 8 [10: 12: 14] rows form stripe sequence – 4 [5: 6: 7] rows using yarn **D** followed by 4 [5: 6: 7] rows using yarn **C**.

Keeping stripes correct as now set, cont as folls:

Inc 1 st at each end of next [3rd: next: next] and 5 [6: 5: 2] foll 4th rows, then on 0 [0: 2: 5] foll 6th rows. 45 [49: 53: 57] sts.

Work 3 rows, ending after 4 [5: 6: 7] rows of 4th stripe using yarn **C** and with RS facing for next row.

Break off yarn **C** and yarn **D** and join in yarn **B**.

Work 2 rows, ending with RS facing for next row.

Shape Raglan

Cast off 3 sts at beg of next row. 42 [46: 50: 54] sts.

Next row (WS): Cast off 3 sts, then cast on 5 sts (for button band underlay), work across these 5 sts as folls: K1, P3, K1, then P to end. 44 [48: 52: 56] sts.

Next row: K2tog, K to last 7 sts, sl 1, K1, psso (for front raglan edge dec), P1, K4.

Next row: K1, P3, K1, P2tog tbl (for front raglan edge dec), P to last 2 sts, P2tog. 40 [44: 48: 52] sts.

Keeping sts correct as now set and working all raglan decreases as set by last 2 rows, cont as folls:

Dec 1 st at both raglan edges of next 3 [3: 5: 5] rows, then on foll 10 [12: 12: 14] alt rows, ending with **WS** facing for next row. 14 sts.

Cast off 7 sts at beg of next row, dec 1 st at beg of foll row, and cast off 3 sts at beg of foll row.

Cast off rem 3 sts.

RIGHT SLEEVE

Work as given for Left Sleeve to beg of raglan shaping.

Shape Raglan

Cast off 3 sts at beg of next 2 rows. 39 [43: 47: 51] sts.

Dec 1 st at each end of next 5 [5: 7: 7] rows, then on foll 9 [11: 11: 13] alt rows. 11 sts.

Work 1 row, ending with RS facing for next row.

Cast off 3 sts at beg and dec 1 st at end of next row.

Work 1 row.

Rep last 2 rows once more.

Cast off rem 3 sts.

MAKING UP

Join both back and right front raglan seams.

Neckband

With RS facing, using 3.25 mm (US 3) needles and yarn **B**, pick up and knit 6 [7: 10: 11] sts down left side of front neck, K across 10 sts on front holder, pick up and knit 6 [7: 10: 11] sts up right side of front neck, and 7 sts from top of right sleeve, K across 18 [20: 22: 24] sts on back holder inc 1 st at centre, then pick up and knit 12 sts from top of left sleeve. 60 [64: 72: 76] sts.

Row 1 (WS): K1, P2, *K2, P2, rep from * to last st, K1.

Row 2: K3, *P2, K2, rep from * to last st, K1.

These 2 rows form rib.

Keeping rib correct, cont as folls:

Work 1 row, ending with RS facing for next row.

Row 4 (RS): K3, yo, P2tog (to make 3rd buttonhole), rib to end.

Work in rib for a further 4 [4: 6: 6] rows, ending with **WS** facing for next row.

Cast off in rib (on **WS**).

At base of left front raglan, join seam for first 2 rows, then neatly sew cast-on edge of left sleeve underlay section in place on inside. Join side and sleeve seams. Slip stitch pocket lining in place to WS. Sew on buttons.

Pin out garment to measurements given and cover with damp cloths and leave to dry naturally. See ball band for washing and further care instructions.

SKILL LEVEL

FELIXA

SIZE

AGE	0-6 months	6-12 months	1-2 years	2-3 years
To fit chest				
	41	46	51	56 cm
	16	18	20	22 in
Actual chest measurement				
	44	49	55	60 cm
	17¼	19¼	21½	23½ in
Full length, from shoulder measured at centre back				
	22	27	32	37 cm
	8½	10½	12½	14½ in
Sleeve length				
	15	17	20	24 cm
	6	6½	8	9½ in

YARN
Jody Long Ciao
3 [4: 4: 5] x 50g balls in Wisteria 018

NEEDLES
1 pair 3.25 mm (no 10) (US 3) needles
1 pair 4 mm (no 8) (US 6) needles

BUTTONS - 1 [1: 1: 1]

TENSION
25 sts and 30 rows to 10 cm (4 in) measured over patt using 4 mm (US 6) needles.

ABBREVIATIONS
See inside front flap

SPECIAL ABBREVIATION
Knot 3 = (P3tog, K3tog, P3tog) all into next 3 sts.

BACK
Using 4 mm (US 6) needles cast on 19 [21: 19: 27] sts.
Work in patt and shape hem edge as folls:
Row 1 (RS): Knit.
Row 2: Cast on 6 [5: 5: 4] sts, P to end. 25 [26: 24: 31] sts.
Row 3: Cast on 6 [5: 5: 4] sts, K2 [2: 1: 4], knot 3, *K3, knot 3, rep from * to last 2 [2: 1: 4] sts, K2 [2: 1: 4]. 31 [31: 29: 35] sts.
Row 4: Cast on 6 [5: 5: 4] sts, P to end. 37 [36: 34: 39] sts.
Row 5: Cast on 6 [5: 5: 4] sts, K to end. 43 [41: 39: 43] sts.
Row 6: Cast on 6 [5: 5: 4] sts, P to end. 49 [46: 44: 47] sts.
Row 7: Cast on 6 [5: 5: 4] sts, K5 [3: 2: 3], knot 3, *K3, knot 3, rep from * to last 5 [3: 2: 3] sts, K5 [3: 2: 3]. 55 [51: 49: 51] sts.
Row 8: Cast on 0 [5: 5: 4] sts, P to end. 55 [56: 54: 55] sts.
Last 8 rows form patt and hem shaping.
Keeping patt correct as now set throughout, cont as folls:

6-12 Months, 1-2 Years and 2-3 Years Only
Cast on [5: 5: 4] sts at beg of next [1: 3: 5] rows, taking cast-on sts into patt. [61: 69: 75] sts.

All Sizes
Work 14 [25: 35: 45] rows, ending with RS facing for next row.

Shape Armholes
Keeping patt correct, cast off 3 sts at beg of next 2 rows. 49 [55: 63: 69] sts.
Dec 1 st at each end of next 3 rows, then on foll 1 [2: 3: 4] alt rows. 41 [45: 51: 55] sts.
Work 23 [21: 25: 27] rows, ending with RS facing for next row.

Shape Shoulders
Keeping patt correct, cast off 4 [5: 6: 6] sts at beg of next 2 rows, then 5 [5: 6: 7] sts at beg of foll 2 rows.

Break yarn and leave rem 23 [25: 27: 29] sts on a holder (for Neckband).

LEFT FRONT

Using 4 mm (US 6) needles cast on 6 [5: 5: 4] sts.

Work in patt and shape hem edge as folls:

Row 1 (RS): Knit.

Row 2: Cast on 6 [5: 5: 4] sts, P to end. 12 [10: 10: 8] sts.

Row 3: K11 [5: 9: 3], (knot 3, K1) 0 [1: 0: 1] times, inc knitwise into last st. 13 [11: 11: 9] sts.

Row 4: Inc **purlwise** into first st, P to end. 14 [12: 12: 10] sts.

Row 5: K2 [11: 6: 9], (knot 3, K3) 1 [0: 0: 0] times, (knot 3, K2) 1 [0: 1: 0] times, inc knitwise into last st. 15 [13: 13: 11] sts.

Row 6: Inc **purlwise** into first st, P to end. 16 [14: 14: 12] sts.

Row 7: K15 [2: 13: 6], (knot 3, K3) 0 [1: 0: 0] times, (knot 3, K2) 0 [1: 0: 1] times, inc knitwise into last st. 17 [15: 15: 13] sts.

Row 8: Inc **purlwise** into first st, P to end. 18 [16: 16: 14] sts.

Last 8 rows for patt and start to shape hem and front opening edge.

Keeping patt correct as now set throughout, cont as folls:

Inc 1 st at shaped front opening edge of next 5 [9: 13: 17] rows, then on foll 1 [4: 4: 5] alt rows, then on 0 [0: 1: 1] foll 4th row, taking inc sts into patt. 24 [29: 34: 37] sts.

Work 1 [1: 3: 7] rows, ending with RS facing for next row.

Shape Armhole

Keeping patt correct, cast off 3 sts at beg and inc 1 [0: 0: 0] st at end of next row. 22 [26: 31: 34] sts.

Work 1 row.

Dec 1 st at armhole edge of next 3 rows, then on foll 1 [2: 3: 4] alt rows **and at same time** inc 1 [1: 0: 0] st at front opening edge of next [next: 0: 0] and 1 [0: 0: 0] foll 4th row. 20 [22: 25: 27] sts.

Work 11 [7: 11: 11] rows, ending with RS facing for next row.

Shape Front Neck

Next row (RS): Patt 15 [17: 19: 21] sts and turn, leave rem 5 [5: 6: 6] sts on a holder (for Neckband).

Keeping patt correct, dec 1 st at neck edge of next 4 rows, then on foll 2 [3: 3: 4] alt rows. 9 [10: 12: 13] sts.

Work 3 rows, ending with RS facing for next row.

Shape Shoulder

Keeping patt correct, cast off 4 [5: 6: 6] sts at beg of next row.

Work 1 row.

Cast off rem 5 [5: 6: 7] sts.

RIGHT FRONT

Using 4 mm (US 6) needles cast on 6 [5: 5: 4] sts.

Work in patt and shape hem edge as folls:

Row 1 (WS): Purl.

Row 2: Cast on 6 [5: 5: 4] sts, work across these cast-on sts and rest of row as folls: (K4, knot 3) 1 [0: 1: 0] times, K5 [10: 3: 8]. 12 [10: 10: 8] sts.

Row 3: Purl.

Row 4: Inc knitwise into first st, (K1, knot 3) 0 [1: 0: 1] times, K to end. 13 [11: 11: 9] sts.

Row 5: P to last st, inc **purlwise** into last st. 14 [12: 12: 10] sts.

Row 6: Inc knitwise into first st, (K2, knot 3) 1 [0: 1: 0] times, (K3, knot 3) 1 [0: 0: 0] times, K2 [11: 6: 9]. 15 [13: 13: 11] sts.

Row 7: P to last st, inc **purlwise** into last st. 16 [14: 14: 12] sts.

Row 8: Inc knitwise into first st, (K2, knot 3) 0 [1: 0: 1] times, (K3, knot 3) 0 [1: 0: 0] times, K15 [2: 13: 6]. 17 [15: 15: 13] sts.

Last 8 rows form patt and start to shape hem and front opening edge.

Keeping patt correct as now set throughout, cont as folls:

Inc 1 st at shaped front opening edge of next 6 [10: 14: 18] rows, then on foll 1 [4: 4: 5] alt rows, then on 0 [0: 1: 1] foll 4th row, taking inc sts into patt. 24 [29: 34: 37] sts.

Work 1 [1: 3: 7] rows, ending with RS facing for next row.

Shape Armhole

Keeping patt correct, work 1 row, inc 1 [0: 0: 0] sts at beg of this row, then cast off 3 sts at beg of foll row. 22 [26: 31: 34] sts.

Dec 1 st at armhole edge of next 3 rows, then on foll 1 [2: 3: 4] alt rows **and at same time** inc 1 [1: 0: 0] st at front opening edge of next [next: 0: 0] and 1 [0: 0: 0] foll 4th row. 20 [22: 25: 27] sts.

Work 11 [7: 11: 11] rows, ending with RS facing for next row.

Shape Front Neck

Next row (RS): Break yarn. Slip first 5 [5: 6: 6] sts onto a holder (for Neckband), rejoin yarn and patt to end. 15 [17: 19: 21] sts.

Keeping patt correct, dec 1 st at neck edge of next 4 rows, then on foll 2 [3: 3: 4] alt rows. 9 [10: 12: 13] sts.

Work 4 rows, ending with **WS** facing for next row.

Shape Shoulder

Keeping patt correct, cast off 4 [5: 6: 6] sts at beg of next row.

Work 1 row.

Cast off rem 5 [5: 6: 7] sts.

SLEEVES

Using 3.25 mm (US 3) needles cast on 27 [29: 31: 33] sts.

Work in g st for 4 [4: 6: 6] rows, ending with RS facing for next row.

Change to 4 mm (US 6) needles.

Now work in patt and shape sleeve as folls:

Row 1 (RS): (Inc knitwise into first st) 1 [0: 0: 0] times, K to last 1 [0: 0: 0] st, (inc knitwise into last st) 1 [0: 0: 0] times. 29 [29: 31: 33] wsts.

Row 2: Purl.

Row 3: (Inc knitwise into first st) 0 [1: 1: 1] times, K1 [0: 1: 2], knot 3, *K3, knot 3, rep from * to last 1 [1: 2: 3] sts, K1 [0: 1: 2], (inc knitwise into last st) 0 [1: 1: 1] times. 29 [31: 33: 35] sts.

Row 4: As row 2.

Row 5: (Inc knitwise into first st) 1 [0: 0: 0] times, K to last 1 [0: 0: 0] st, (inc knitwise into last st) 1 [0: 0: 0] times. 31 [31: 33: 35] sts.

Row 6: As row 2.

Row 7: (Inc knitwise into first st) 0 [1: 1: 1] times, K5 [4: 5: 0], knot 3, *K3, knot 3, rep from * to last 5 [5: 6: 1] sts, K5 [4: 5: 0], (inc knitwise into last st) 0 [1: 1: 1] times. 31 [33: 35: 37] sts.

Row 8: Purl

These 8 rows **set position** of patt as given for Back and start sleeve increases.

Keeping patt correct as now set, inc 1 st at each end of next [3rd: 3rd: 3rd] and every foll 4th row to 47 [51: 55: 55] sts, then on 0 [0: 0: 2] foll 6th rows. 47 [51: 55: 59] sts.

Cont straight until Sleeve meas 15 [17: 20: 24] cm (6 [6¾: 8: 9½] in), ending with RS facing for next row.

Shape Top

Keeping patt correct, cast off 3 sts at beg of next 2 rows. 41 [45: 49: 53] sts.

Dec 1 st at each end of next 5 rows, then on foll 4 alt rows, then on foll 5 [7: 9: 11] rows, ending with RS facing for next row.

Cast off rem 13 sts.

MAKING UP

Join both shoulder seams.

Front and Hem Trim

Using 3.25 mm (US 3) needles cast on 4 sts.

Row 1 (WS): Inc **purlwise** once into each st. 8 sts.

Now work in border patt as folls:

Row 1 (RS): Sl 1, K2, yo, K2tog, K1, (yo) 4 times, K2. 12 sts.

Row 2: Sl 1, K1, (K1, P1, K1, P1) into (yo) 4 times of previous row, K3, yo, K2tog, K1.

Row 3: Sl 1, K2, yo, K2tog, K7.

Row 4: Sl 1, K8, yo, K2tog, K1.

Row 5: As row 3.

Row 6: Cast off 4 sts **knitwise**, K to last 3 sts, yo, K2tog, K1. 8 sts.

These 6 rows form patt.

Cont in patt until straight row-end edge of Trim fits neatly down entire right front opening and hem edge, from neck shaping to side seam, across shaped back hem edge, and up entire left front hem and front opening edge to neck shaping, ending with patt row 6 and RS facing for next row.

Break yarn and leave rem 8 sts on a holder (for Neckband).

Neatly sew Trim in place.

Neckband

With RS facing and using 3.25 mm (US 3) needles, pick up and knit 4 sts from cast-on edge of Front and Hem Trim, K across 5 [5: 6: 6] sts on right front holder, pick up and knit 12 [14: 14: 16] sts up right side of front neck, K across 23 [25: 27: 29] sts on back holder, pick up and knit 12 [14: 14: 16] sts down left side of front neck, K across 5 [5: 6: 6] sts on left front holder, then work across 8 sts of Trim holder as folls: (K2tog) 4 times. 65 [71: 75: 81] sts.

Work in g st for 1 row, ending with RS facing for next row.

Row 2 (RS): K3, K2tog, yo (to make a buttonhole), K to end.

Work in g st for a further 2 rows, ending with **WS** facing for next row.

Cast off **knitwise** (on **WS**).

Join side seams. Join sleeve seams. Sew sleeves into armholes. Sew on button.

Pin out garment to measurements given and cover with damp cloths and leave to dry naturally. See ball band for washing and further care instructions.

GINA

SIZES

AGE	0-6 months	6-12 months	1-2 years	2-3 years
Measurement around lower edge				
	34	36	38	40 cm
	13½	14¼	15	15¾ in

YARN

Jody Long Ciao

A 1 [1: 1: 1] x 50g balls in Cornflower 009
B 1 [1: 1: 1] x 50g balls in Alabaster 002
C 1 [1: 1: 1] x 50g balls in Petal 020

NEEDLES

1 pair 3.25 mm (no 10) (US 3) needles
1 pair 4 mm (no 8) (US 6) needles

TENSION

22 sts and 30 rows to 10 cm (4 in) measured over st st using 4 mm (US 6) needles.

ABBREVIATIONS

See inside front flap

BERET

Using 3.25 mm (US 3) needles and yarn **A** cast on 82 [86: 90: 98] sts.
Row 1 (RS): K2, *P2, K2, rep from * to end.
Row 2: P2, *K2, P2, rep from * to end.
These 2 rows form rib.
Cont in rib for a further 5 [5: 7: 7] rows, ending with **WS** facing for next row.
Next row (WS): P4 [3: 5: 3], P2tog, (P10 [11: 11: 7], P2tog) 6 [6: 6: 10] times, P4 [3: 5: 3]. 75 [79: 83: 87] sts.
Change to 4 mm (US 6) needles.
Beg with a K row, work in striped st st as folls:
Rows 1 and 2: Using yarn **B**, work 2 rows.
Rows 3 and 4: Using yarn **C**, work 2 rows.
These 4 rows form striped st st.
Keeping stripes correct, work as folls:
Row 5 (RS): K2 [4: 3: 2], M1, (K5, M1) 14 [14: 15: 16] times, K3 [5: 5: 5]. 90 [94: 99: 104] sts.
Work 3 rows.
Row 9: K2 [4: 3: 2], M1, (K6, M1) 14 [14: 15: 16] times, K4 [6: 6: 6]. 105 [109: 115: 121] sts.
Work 3 rows.
Row 13: K2 [4: 3: 2], M1, (K7, M1) 14 [14: 15: 16] times, K5 [7: 7: 7]. 120 [124: 131: 138] sts.
Work 3 rows.
Row 17: K2 [4: 3: 2], M1, (K8, M1) 14 [14: 15: 16], K6 [8: 8: 8]. 135 [139: 147: 155] sts.
Cont straight in striped st st, until Beret meas 11 cm (4¼ in), ending with **WS** [**WS**: **WS**: RS] facing for next row.

0-6 Months Only
Next row (WS): P67, P2tog, P66. 134 sts.

6-12 Months Only
Next row (WS): P35, M1P, P69, M1P, P35. [141] sts.

1-2 Years Only
Next row (WS): P73, M1P, P74. [148] sts.

All Sizes
Shape Crown
Next row (RS): K1, *K2tog, K5, rep from * to end. 115 [121: 127: 133] sts.
Work 3 [5: 5: 5] rows.
Next row: K1, *K2tog, K4, rep from * to end. 96 [101: 106: 111] sts.
Work 3 [5: 5: 5] rows.
Next row: K1, *K2tog, K3, rep from * to end. 77 [81: 85: 89] sts.
Work 3 [3: 3: 5] rows.
Next row: K1, *K2tog, K2, rep from * to end. 58 [61: 64: 67] sts.
Work 3 rows.
Next row: K1, *K2tog, K1, rep from * to end. 39 [41: 43: 45] sts.
Work 1 row.
Next row: K1, *K2tog, rep from * to end. 20 [21: 22: 23] sts.
Next row: (P2tog) 10 [10: 11: 11] times, P0 [1: 0: 1].
Break off yarn and thread through rem 10 [11: 11: 12] sts, pull up tightly and fasten off securely.

BOW

Using 3.25 mm (US 3) needles and yarn **C** cast on 7 [7: 9: 9] sts.
Row 1 (RS): K1, *P1, K1, rep from * to end.
Row 2: As row 1.
These 2 rows form moss st.
Work a further 30 [30: 36: 36] rows in moss st, ending with RS facing for next row.
Cast off in patt.

BOW CENTRE

Using 3.25 mm (US 3) needles and yarn **C** cast on 8 [8: 9: 9] sts.
Beg with a K row, work 3 rows in st st, ending with **WS** facing for next row.
Cast off **knitwise** (on **WS**).

MAKING UP

Join centre back seam of beret by joining row-ends together.
Join row-ends of bow centre around centre of moss st strip to form a bow shape as shown in photograph. Attach the bow to ribbing of beret as shown.
Cover with damp cloths and leave to dry naturally. See ball band for washing and further care instructions.

LENA

SIZES

AGE	0-6 months	6-12 months	1-2 years	2-3 years
To fit chest				
	41	46	51	56 cm
	16	18	20	22 in
Actual chest measurement				
	47	52	57	62 cm
	18½	20½	22½	24½ in
Full length, from shoulder				
	22	23	26	29 cm
	8½	9	10¼	11½ in
Sleeve length				
	3	3	4	4 cm
	1¼	1¼	1½	1½ in

YARN
Jody Long Ciao
2 [3: 3: 4] x 50g balls in Dijon 016

NEEDLES
1 pair 3.25 mm (no 10) (US 3) needles
1 pair 4 mm (no 8) (US 6) needles

BUTTONS - 3 [3: 3: 3]

TENSION
24 sts and 29 rows to 10 cm (4 in) measured over pattern using 4 mm (US 6) needles.

ABBREVIATIONS
See inside front flap

PATTERN NOTE: When working patt from chart, ensure each increase of patt is matched by a decrease. If there are insufficient sts to work both, work end sts of rows in st st.

BACK
Using 3.25 mm (US 3) needles cast on 56 [62: 68: 74] sts.
Row 1 (RS): K0 [0: 1: 0], P1 [0: 2: 2], *K2, P2, rep from * to last 3 [2: 1: 0] sts, K2 [2: 1: 0], P1 [0: 0: 0].
Row 2: P0 [0: 1: 0], K1 [0: 2: 2], *P2, K2, rep from * to last 3 [2: 1: 0] sts, P2 [2: 1: 0], K1 [0: 0: 0].
These 2 rows form rib.
Work in rib for a further 8 [8: 10: 10] rows, ending with RS facing for next row.
Change to 4 mm (US 6) needles.
Beg and ending rows as indicated and repeating the 6 row patt repeat throughout, now work in patt from chart (see pattern note) as folls:
Cont straight until Back meas 12 [12: 14: 16] cm (4¾ [4¾: 5½: 6¼] in), ending with RS facing for next row.

Shape Armholes
Keeping patt correct, cast off 3 sts at beg of next 2 rows. 50 [56: 62: 68] sts.
Dec 1 st at each end of next 3 [3: 3: 5] rows, then on foll 3 [3: 4: 3] alt rows. 38 [44: 48: 52] sts.
Cont straight until armhole meas 10 [11: 12: 13] cm (4 [4¼: 4¾: 5] in), ending with RS facing for next row.

Shape Shoulders
Cast off 4 [5: 5: 6] sts at beg of next 2 rows, then 5 [6: 6: 6] sts at beg of foll 2 rows.

Break yarn and leave rem 20 [22: 26: 28] sts on a holder (for Neckband).

LEFT FRONT

Using 3.25 mm (US 3) needles cast on 28 [31: 34: 37] sts.

Row 1 (RS): K0 [0: 1: 0], P1 [0: 2: 2], *K2, P2, rep from * to last 3 sts, K3.

Row 2: K1, *P2, K2, rep from * to last 3 [2: 1: 0] sts, P2 [2: 1: 0], K1 [0: 0: 0].

These 2 rows form rib.

Work in rib for a further 8 [8: 10: 10] rows, ending with RS facing for next row.

Change to 4 mm (US 6) needles.

Beg and ending rows as indicated and repeating the 6 row patt repeat throughout, now work in patt from chart (see pattern note) as folls:

Cont straight until Left Front matches Back to beg of armhole shaping, ending with RS facing for next row.

Shape Armhole

Keeping patt correct, cast off 3 sts at beg of next row. 25 [28: 31: 34] sts.

Work 1 row.

Dec 1 st at armhole edge of next 3 [3: 3: 5] rows, then on foll 3 [3: 4: 3] alt rows. 19 [22: 24: 26] sts.

Cont straight until 12 [12: 14: 14] rows less have been worked than on Back to beg of shoulder shaping, ending with RS facing for next row.

Shape Front Neck

Next Row (RS): Patt 16 [18: 19: 20] sts and turn, leaving rem 3 [4: 5: 6] sts on a holder (for Neckband).

Keeping patt correct, dec 1 st at neck edge of next 4 rows, then on foll 3 [3: 4: 4] alt rows. 9 [11: 11: 12] sts.

Work 1 row, ending with RS facing for next row.

Shape Shoulder

Cast off 4 [5: 5: 6] sts at beg of next row.

Work 1 row.

Cast off rem 5 [6: 6: 6] sts.

RIGHT FRONT

Using 3.25 mm (US 3) needles cast on 28 [31: 34: 37] sts.

Row 1 (RS): K1, *K2, P2, rep from * to last 3 [2: 1: 0] sts, K2 [2: 1: 0], P1 [0: 0: 0].

Row 2: P0 [0: 1: 0], K1 [0: 2: 2], *P2, K2, rep from * to last 3 sts, P2, K1.

These 2 rows form rib.

Work in rib for a further 8 [8: 10: 10] rows, ending with RS facing for next row.

Change to 4 mm (US 6) needles.

Beg and ending rows as indicated and repeating the 6 row patt repeat throughout, now work in patt from chart (see pattern note) as folls:

Cont straight until Right Front matches Back to beg of armhole shaping, ending with RS facing for next row.

Shape Armhole

Work 1 row.

Keeping patt correct, cast off 3 sts at beg of next row. 25 [28: 31: 34] sts.

Dec 1 st at armhole edge of next 3 [3: 3: 5] rows, then on foll 3 [3: 4: 3] alt rows. 19 [22: 24: 26] sts.

Cont straight until 12 [12: 14: 14] rows less have been worked than on Back to beg of shoulder shaping, ending with RS facing for next row.

Shape Front Neck

Next Row (RS): K3, P0 [1: 2: 2], K0 [0: 0: 1] and slip these 3 [4: 5: 6] sts onto a holder (for Neckband), patt to end. 16 [18: 19: 20] sts.

Keeping patt correct, dec 1 st at neck edge of next 4 rows, then on foll 3 [3: 4: 4] alt rows. 9 [11: 11: 12] sts.

Work 2 rows, ending with **WS** facing for next row.

Shape Shoulder

Cast off 4 [5: 5: 6] sts at beg of next row.

Work 1 row.

Cast off rem 5 [6: 6: 6] sts.

SLEEVES

Using 3.25 mm (US 3) needles cast on 46 [50: 56: 60] sts.

Row 1 (RS): K0 [0: 0: 1], P0 [2: 1: 2], *K2, P2, rep from * to last 2 [0: 3: 1] sts, K2 [0: 2: 1], P0 [0: 1: 0].

Row 2: P0 [0: 0: 1], K0 [2: 1: 2], *P2, K2, rep from * to last 2 [0: 3: 1] sts, P2 [0: 2: 1], K0 [0: 1: 0].

These 2 rows form rib.

Work in rib for a further 4 [4: 6: 6] rows, ending with RS facing for next row.

Change to 4 mm (US 6) needles.

Beg and ending rows as indicated and repeating the 6 row patt repeat throughout, now work in patt from chart (see pattern note) as folls:

Cont straight until Sleeve meas 3 [3: 4: 4] cm (1¼ [1¼: 1½: 1½] in), ending with RS facing for next row.

Shape Top

Keeping patt correct, cast off 3 sts at beg of next 2 rows. 40 [44: 50: 54] sts.

Dec 1 st at each end of next 5 rows, then on foll 3 [4: 4: 5] alt rows, then on foll 7 [7: 9: 9] rows, ending with RS facing for next row.

Cast off rem 10 [12: 14: 16] sts.

MAKING UP

Join both shoulder seams.

Neckband

With RS facing and using 3.25 mm (US 3) needles, slip 3 [4: 5: 6] sts on right front holder onto right needle, pick up and knit 13 [13: 14: 14] sts up right side of front neck, K across 20 [22: 26: 28] sts on back holder, pick up and knit 13 [13: 14: 14] sts down left side of front neck, then work across 3 [4: 5: 6] sts on left front holder as folls: K0 [0: 0: 1], P0 [1: 2: 2], K3. 52 [56: 64: 68] sts.

Row 1 (WS): K1, P2, *K2, P2, rep from * to last st, K1.

Row 2: K3, *P2, K2, rep from * to last st, K1.

These 2 rows form rib.

Work in rib for a further 3 [3: 5: 5] rows, ending with RS facing for next row.

Cast off in rib.

Button Band

With RS facing and using 3.25 mm (US 3) needles, pick up and knit 48 [52: 60: 68] sts evenly down left front opening edge, from top of Neckband to cast-on edge.

Beg with row 1, work in rib as given for Neckband for 5 rows, ending with RS facing for next row.

Cast off in rib.

Buttonhole Band

With RS facing and using 3.25 mm (US 3) needles, pick up and knit 48 [52: 60: 68] sts evenly up right front opening edge, from cast-on edge to top of Neckband.

Beg with row 1, work in rib as given for Neckband for 2 rows, ending with **WS** facing for next row.

Row 3 (WS): Rib 2, *work 2 tog, yo (to make a buttonhole), rib 5 [6: 7: 8], rep from * once more, work 2 tog, yo (to make 3rd buttonhole), rib to end.

Work in rib for a further 2 rows, ending with RS facing for next row. Cast off in rib.

Join side seams. Join sleeve seams. Insert sleeves into armholes. Sew on buttons.

Pin out garment to measurements given and cover with damp cloths and leave to dry naturally. See ball band for washing and further care instructions.

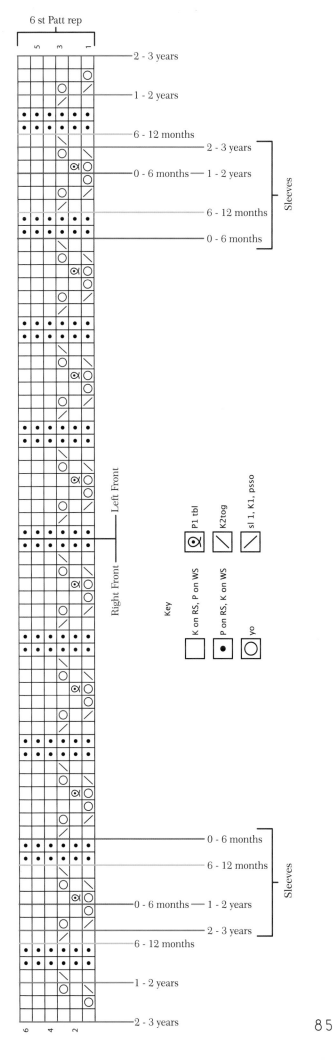

6 st Patt rep

Left Front

Right Front

Sleeves — 2 - 3 years, 1 - 2 years, 6 - 12 months, 0 - 6 months

Sleeves — 0 - 6 months, 6 - 12 months, 1 - 2 years, 2 - 3 years

Key

	P1 tbl
	K2tog
	sl 1, K1, psso
	K on RS, P on WS
•	P on RS, K on WS
○	yo

LEONARDO

SIZES

AGE	0-6 months	6-12 months	1-2 years	2-3 years
To fit chest				
	41	46	51	56 cm
	16	18	20	22 in
Actual chest measurement				
	47	53	59	63 cm
	18½	20¾	23¼	24¾ in
Full length, from back neck				
	23	28	33	38 cm
	9½	11	12½	15 in
Sleeve length				
	15	17	20	24 cm
	6	6½	8	9½ in

YARN

Jody Long Ciao
4 [5: 6: 7] x 50g balls in Marine 008 or Chrome 004

NEEDLES

1 pair 3.75 mm (no 9) (US 5) needles
1 pair 4 mm (no 8) (US 6) needles

BUTTONS - 6 [6: 7: 7]

TENSION

21 sts and 39 rows to 10 cm (4 in) measured over g st using 4 mm (US 6) needles.

ABBREVIATIONS

See inside front flap

BACK

Using 3.75 mm (US 5) needles cast on 47 [53: 59: 63] sts.
Work in g st for 2 rows, ending with RS facing for next row.
Change to 4 mm (US 6) needles.
Cont in g st for a further 82 [100: 120: 138] rows, ending with RS facing for next row.

Shape Shoulders

Cast off 5 [6: 6: 7] sts at beg of next 4 [6: 2: 4] rows, then 6 [-: 7: 8] sts at beg of foll 2 [-: 4: 2] rows.
Break yarn and leave rem 15 [17: 19: 19] sts on a holder (for Neckband).

LEFT FRONT

Using 3.75 mm (US 5) needles cast on 26 [29: 32: 34] sts.
Work in g st for 2 rows, ending with RS facing for next row.
Change to 4 mm (US 6) needles.
Cont in g st for a further 2 rows, ending with RS facing for next row.
Next row (RS): K to last 5 sts, K2tog, yo (to make a buttonhole) K3.
Work in g st for 19 [25: 23: 27] rows, ending with RS facing for next row.
Rep the last 20 [26: 24: 28] rows 2 [2: 3: 3] times more, ending with RS facing for next row.
Next row (RS): K to last 5 sts, K2tog, yo (to make 4th [4th: 5th: 5th] buttonhole) K3.
Cont in g st for 3 rows, ending with RS facing for next row.

Shape Front Neck

Work 1 row.
Cast off 5 sts at beg of next row. 21 [24: 27: 29] sts.

Dec 1 st at neck edge of next 3 [5: 5: 5] rows, then on foll 2 [1: 2: 1] alt rows, then on foll 0 [0: 0: 1] 4th row. 16 [18: 20: 22] sts.
Work 7 rows, ending with RS facing for next row.

Shape Shoulders
Cast off 5 [6: 6: 7] sts at beg of next row, then 5 [6: 7: 7] sts at beg of foll alt row.
Work 1 row.
Cast off rem 6 [6: 7: 8] sts.

RIGHT FRONT
Using 3.75 mm (US 5) needles cast on 26 [29: 32: 34] sts.
Work in g st for 2 rows, ending with RS facing for next row.
Change to 4 mm (US 6) needles.
Cont in g st for a further 66 [84: 102: 118] rows, ending with RS facing for next row.

Shape Front Neck
Cast off 5 sts at beg of next row. 21 [24: 27: 29] sts.
Work 1 row.
Dec 1 st at neck edge of next 3 [5: 5: 5] rows, then on foll 2 [1: 2: 1] alt rows, then on foll 0 [0: 0: 1] 4th row. 16 [18: 20: 22] sts.
Work 7 rows, ending with RS facing for next row.

Shape Shoulders
Work 1 row.
Cast off 5 [6: 6: 7] sts at beg of next row, then 5 [6: 7: 7] sts at beg of foll alt row.
Work 1 row.
Cast off rem 6 [6: 7: 8] sts.

SLEEVES
Using 3.75 mm (US 5) needles cast on 29 [29: 31: 31] sts.
Work in g st for 2 rows, ending with RS facing for next row.
Change to 4 mm (US 6) needles.
Cont in g st as folls:
Inc 1 st at each end of 5th [3rd: 3rd: 3rd] and every foll 8th [6th: 6th: 6th] row until there are 41 [41: 47: 47] sts, then on - [2: 2: 4] foll - [8th: 8th: 8th] rows. 41 [45: 51: 55] sts.
Cont straight until Sleeve meas 15 [17: 20: 24] cm (6 [6¾: 8: 9½] in), ending with RS facing for next row.

Shape Top
Cast off 2 sts at beg of next 14 [10: 4: 8] rows, then 3 sts at beg of foll 2 [6: 12: 10] rows.
Cast off rem 7 [7: 7: 9] sts.

POCKETS (Make 2)
Using 4 mm (US 6) needles cast on 17 [17: 19: 19] sts.
Beg with a K row, work in st st for 19 [19: 21: 21] rows, ending with **WS** facing for next row.
Cast off **knitwise** (on **WS**).

EPAULETTES (Make 2)
Using 3.75 mm (US 5) needles cast on 9 [9: 11: 11] sts.
Work 2 rows in g st, ending with RS facing for next row.
Next row (RS): Knit.
Next row: K2, P to last 2 sts, K2.

Rep the last 2 rows 10 [11: 11: 13] times, ending with RS facing for next row.
Work 3 rows in g st.
Cast off **knitwise** (on **WS**).

MAKING UP
Join both shoulder seams.

Collar
Starting halfway across cast-off sts at Right Front side of neck edge and with RS facing, using 4 mm (US 6) needles, pick up and knit 18 [18: 20: 22] sts up right side of front neck, K across 15 [17: 19: 19] sts on back holder, pick up and knit 18 [18: 20: 22] sts down left side of front neck finishing halfway across cast-off sts at neck edge. 51 [53: 59: 63] sts.
Next row (RS): K8 [9: 9: 9], inc knitwise into next st, (K4, inc knitwise into next st) 7 [7: 8: 9] times, K7 [8: 9: 8]. 59 [61: 68: 73]sts.
Work in g st for 21 [23: 25: 27] rows, ending with RS facing for next row.
Next row (RS): K17 [18: 21: 24], inc knitwise into next st, (K2, inc knitwise into next st) 8 times, K17 [18: 22: 24]. 68 [70: 77: 82] sts.
Cast off **loosely** (on **WS**).
Mark points along side seam edges 11 [12: 13: 14] cm (4¼ [4¾: 5: 5½] in) either side of shoulder seams, then sew shaped cast-off edge of sleeve to back and front between these points. Join side and sleeve seams. Sew on buttons. Sew on pockets as shown in photograph with cast-on edge of pocket on 5th row of each front with edge of pocket starting on 4th [4th: 5th: 5th] st in from side seam of fronts. Sew cast-on edge of epaulettes to each shoulder at neck edge, sew on buttons to outside of each epaulette, sewing through both layers epaulette and shoulder seam as shown in photograph.
Pin out garment to measurements given and cover with damp cloths and leave to dry naturally. See ball band for washing and further care instructions.

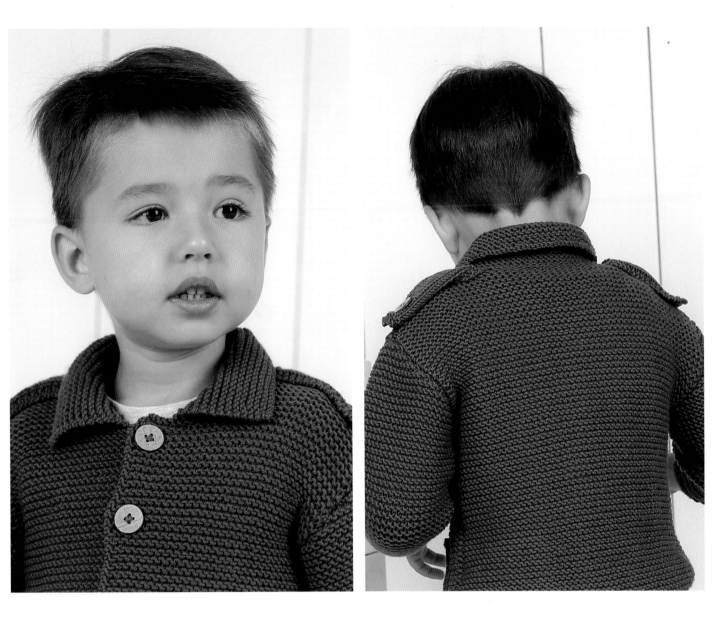

SKILL LEVEL

LORENZO

SIZES

YARN
Jody Long Ciao
3 [4: 4: 5] x 50g balls in Nougat 007

NEEDLES
1 pair 3.25 mm (no 10) (US 3) needles
1 pair 4 mm (no 8) (US 6) needles

BUTTONS - 2 [2: 2: 2]

TENSION
23 sts and 30 rows to 10 cm (4 in) measured over patt using 4 mm (US 6) needles.

ABBREVIATIONS
See inside front flap

BACK
Using 3.25 mm (US 3) needles cast on 54 [60: 66: 72] sts.
Work in g st for 6 [6: 8: 8] rows, ending with RS facing for next row.
Change to 4 mm (US 6) needles.
Next row (RS): Knit.
Next row: K2 [2: 5: 5], *P2, K1, rep from * to last 4 [4: 7: 7] sts, P2, K2 [2: 5: 5].
These 2 rows set the sts – 2 [2: 5: 5] sts still in g st at each end of rows and all other sts now in patt.
Cont as now set for a further 6 [6: 10: 10] rows, ending with RS facing for next row.
Place markers at both ends of last row (to denote top of side seam openings).
Now working **all** sts in patt, cont as folls:
Cont straight until Back meas 24 [28: 32: 38] cm (9½ [11: 12½: 15] in), ending with RS facing for next row.

Shape Shoulders
Cast off 8 [9: 10: 11] sts at beg of next 4 rows.
Break yarn and leave rem 22 [24: 26: 28] sts on a holder (for Neckband).

FRONT
Work as given for Back until 34 [38: 44: 46] rows less have been worked than on Back to beg of shoulder shaping, ending with RS facing for next row.

Divide for Front Opening
Next row (RS): K29 [32: 35: 38] and turn, leaving rem sts on a holder.
Work on this set of sts only for first side of neck as folls:
Next row (WS): K4, patt to end.

This row sets the sts – front opening edge 4 sts in g st with all other sts still in patt.

Cont as now set for a further 8 [10: 12: 12] rows, ending with RS facing for next row.

Next row (RS): K to last 3 sts, yo, K2tog (to make first buttonhole), K1.

Work a further 11 [11: 13: 15] rows, ending with RS facing for next row.

Shape Front Neck

Next row (RS): K22 [25: 28: 30] and turn, leaving rem 7 [7: 7: 8] sts on another holder (for Neckband).

Keeping patt correct, dec 1 st at neck edge of next 4 rows, then on foll 2 [3: 4: 4] alt rows. 16 [18: 20: 22] sts.

Work 3 rows, ending with RS facing for next row.

Shape Shoulder

Cast off 8 [9: 10: 11] sts at beg of next row.

Work 1 row.

Cast off rem 8 [9: 10: 11] sts.

Return to sts left on first holder and rejoin yarn with RS facing, pick up and knit 4 sts from behind 4 sts in g st up left front opening edge (or cast on 4 sts if preferred), K to end. 29 [32: 35: 38] sts.

Next row (WS): Patt to last 4 sts, K4.

This row sets the sts – front opening edge 4 sts in g st with all other sts still in patt.

Cont as now set for a further 21 [23: 27: 29] rows, ending with RS facing for next row.

Shape Front Neck

Next row (RS): K7 [7: 7: 8] and slip these sts onto another holder (for Neckband), K to end. 22 [25: 28: 30] sts.

Keeping patt correct, dec 1 st at neck edge of next 4 rows, then on foll 2 [3: 4: 4] alt rows. 16 [18: 20: 22] sts.

Work 4 rows, ending with **WS** facing for next row.

Shape Shoulder

Cast off 8 [9: 10: 11] sts at beg of next row.

Work 1 row.

Cast off rem 8 [9: 10: 11] sts.

SLEEVES

Using 3.25 mm (US 3) needles cast on 29 [31: 33: 35] sts.

Work in g st for 6 [6: 8: 8] rows, ending with RS facing for next row.

Change to 4 mm (US 6) needles.

Next row (RS): Knit.

Next row: P2 [0: 1: 2], K1, *P2, K1, rep from * to last 2 [0: 1: 2] sts, P2 [0: 1: 2].

These 2 rows form patt.

Cont in patt, shaping sides by inc 1 st at each end of next and every foll 4th row to 35 [43: 47: 43] sts, then on every foll 6th row until there are 41 [47: 51: 55] sts, taking inc sts into patt.

Cont straight until Sleeve meas 15 [17: 20: 24] cm (6 [6¾: 8: 9½] in), ending with RS facing for next row.

Shape Top

Keeping patt correct, cast off 7 [8: 8: 9] sts at beg of next 2 rows, then 7 [8: 9: 9] sts at beg of foll 2 rows.

Cast off rem 13 [15: 17: 19] sts.

MAKING UP

Join both shoulder seams.

Neckband

With RS facing and using 3.25 mm (US 3) needles, slip 7 [7: 7: 8] sts on right front holder onto right needle, rejoin yarn and pick up and knit 10 [12: 14: 14] sts up right side of front neck, K across 22 [24: 26: 28] sts on back holder, pick up and knit 10 [12: 14: 14] sts down left side of front neck, then K across 7 [7: 7: 8] sts on left front holder. 56 [62: 68: 72] sts.

Row 1 (WS): Knit.

Row 2: K to last 3 sts, yo, K2tog (to make second buttonhole), K1.

Work in g st for a further 2 rows, ending with **WS** facing for next row.

Cast off **knitwise** (on **WS**).

If required, at base of front opening, neatly sew cast-on edge in place behind left front opening edge. Mark points along side seam edges 10 [11: 12: 13] cm (4 [4¼: 4¾: 5] in) either side of shoulder seams, then sew shaped cast-off edge of sleeve to back and front between these points. Join side and sleeve seams, leaving side seams open below markers (for side seam openings). Sew on buttons.

Pin out garment to measurements given, cover with damp cloths and leave to dry naturally. See ball band for washing and further care instructions.

Front

Back

BELLA

SIZE
Completed blanket measured 85 cm (33½ in) wide and 103 cm (40½ in) long.

YARN
Jody Long Ciao
12 x 50g balls in Nougat 007

NEEDLES
3.25 mm (no 10) (US 3) circular needle
4 mm (no 8) (US 6) circular needle

TENSION
21½ sts and 35 rows to 10 cm (4 in) measured over patt using 4 mm (US 6) needles.

ABBREVIATIONS
See inside front flap

BLANKET
Using 3.25 mm (US 3) circular needle cast on 182 sts.
Working back and forth in rows not rounds, work as folls:
Work 14 rows in g st, ending with RS facing for next row.
Change to 4 mm (US 6) circular needle.
Now work in patt as folls:
Row 1 (RS): Knit.
Row 2: K6, P2, *(K1, P1) 3 times, P1, rep from * to last 6 sts, K6.
Row 3: K8, *(K1, P1) twice, K3, rep from * to last 6 sts, K6.
Rows 4 to 7: As rows 2 to 3 twice.
Row 8: K6, *P2, K12, rep from * to last 8 sts, P2, K6.
Row 9: K8, *P12, K2, rep from * to last 6 sts, K6.
Row 10: K6, P to last 6 sts, K6.
Row 11: K8, *(P1, K1) 3 times, K1, rep from * to last 6 sts, K6.
Row 12: K6, *P3, (K1, P1) twice, rep from * to last 8 sts, P2, K6.
Rows 13 to 16: As rows 11 and 12 twice.
Row 17: K6, P7, *K2, P12, rep from * to last 15 sts, K2, P7, K6.
Row 18: K13, *P2, K12, rep from * to last 15 sts, P2, K13.
These 18 rows form patt.
Cont in patt until Blanket meas approx 100 cm (39½ in), ending with row 16 and RS facing for next row.
Change to 3.25 mm (US 3) circular needle.
Work 13 rows in g st, ending with **WS** facing for next row.
Cast off **knitwise** (on **WS**).

MAKING UP
Pin out to measurements given and cover with damp cloths and leave to dry naturally. See ball band for washing and further care instructions.

ROCCO

SIZES

AGE	0-6 months	6-12 months	1-2 years	2-3 years
To fit chest				
	41	46	51	56 cm
	16	18	20	22 in
Length from shoulder to wrist				
	20	24	28	32 cm
	8	9½	11	12½ in

YARN
Jody Long Ciao
6 [6: 7: 8] x 50g balls in Poppy 014

NEEDLES
1 pair 3.25 mm (no 10) (US 3) needles
1 pair 4 mm (no 8) (US 6) needles
Cable needle

TENSION
30 sts and 30 rows to 10 cm (4 in) measured over patt using 4 mm (US 6) needles.

ABBREVIATIONS
See inside front flap

SPECIAL ABBREVIATIONS
C4B = slip next 2 sts onto cable needle and leave at back of work, K2, then K2 from cable needle.
C4F = slip next 2 sts onto cable needle and leave at front of work, K2, then K2 from cable needle.

PONCHO
Using 3.25 mm (US 3) needles cast on 64 [72: 86: 94] sts.
Row 1 (RS): Knit.
Row 2: Purl.
Row 3: P2 [2: 4: 3], (inc **purlwise** into next st, P1, inc **purlwise** into next st, P2) 12 [14: 16: 18] times, P2 [0: 2: 1]. 88 [100: 118: 130] sts
Change to 4 mm (US 6) needles.
Next row (WS): K4 [3: 3: 2], (P4, K3) 0 [1: 1: 2] times, *P8, K3, P4, K3, rep from * to last 12 [0: 0: 6] sts, (P8, K4) 1 [0: 0: 0] times, (P4, K2) 0 [0: 0: 1] times.
Now work in patt as folls:
Row 1 (RS): P4 [3: 3: 2], (C4F, P3) 0 [1: 1: 2] times, *C4B, (C4F, P3) twice, rep from * to last 12 [0: 0: 6] sts, (C4B, C4F, P4) 1 [0: 0: 0] times, (C4F, P2) 0 [0: 0: 1] times.
Row 2: K4 [3: 3: 2], (P4, K3) 0 [1: 1: 2] times, *P8, K3, P4, K3, rep from * to last 12 [0: 0: 6] sts, (P8, K4) 1 [0: 0: 0] times, (P4, K2) [0: 0: 1] times.
Row 3: P4 [3: 3: 2], (K4, P3) 0 [1: 1: 2] times, *K8, P3, K4, P3, rep from * to last 12 [0: 0: 6] sts, (K8, P4) 1 [0: 0: 0] times, (K4, P2) 0 [0: 0: 1] times.
Row 4: As row 2.
These 4 rows form patt.
Cont in patt until work meas approx 20 [24: 28: 32] cm (8 [9½: 11: 12½] in), ending with row **1** of patt and **WS** facing for next row.

Shape Neck
Keeping patt correct, cast off 18 [18: 22: 22] sts, patt to end. 70 [82: 96: 108] sts.
Dec 1 st at neck edge of next 8 [8: 10: 10] rows. 62 [74: 86: 98] sts.
Work 20 [20: 24: 24] rows without shaping, ending with RS row facing for next row. Place a marker at each end of last row to mark shoulder

Work 20 [20: 24: 24] rows more without shaping, ending with RS row facing for next row.

Inc 1 st at neck edge of next 8 [8: 10: 10] rows, taking inc sts into patt. 70 [82: 96: 108] sts.

Next row (RS): Patt to end, then cast on 18 [18: 22: 22] sts. 88 [100: 118: 130] sts.

Beg with a patt row **2** or **4**, work in patt until the same number of rows have been work before the neck shaping, ending with **WS** facing for next row.

Change to 3.25 mm (US 3) needles.

Row 1 (WS): K2 [2: 4: 3], (K2tog, K1, K2tog, K2) 12 [14: 16: 18] times, K2 [0: 2: 1]. 64 [72: 86: 94] sts.

Row 2: Knit.

Row 3: Purl.

Cast off **purlwise** (on RS).

MAKING UP

Neckband

With RS facing using 3.25 mm (US 3) needless, pick up and knit 17 [17: 21: 21] sts evenly along cast-on sts of neck, 9 [9: 11: 11] sts along shaped edge, 38 [38: 46: 46] sts along straight edge, 9 [9: 11: 11] sts along shaped edge, then 17 [17: 21: 21] sts from cast-off sts. 90 [90: 110: 110] sts.

Row 1 (WS): P2, *K2, P2, rep from * to end.

Row 2: K2, *P2, K2, rep from * to end.

These 2 rows form rib.

Work a further 7 rows in rib, ending with RS facing for next row.

Cast off **loosely** in rib.

Side Edging

With RS facing using 3.25 mm (US 3) needles, pick up and knit 125 [139: 163: 181] sts evenly along straight side edge.

Row 1 (WS): Knit.

Row 2: Knit.

Row 3: Purl.

Cast off **purlwise** (on RS).

Fold poncho in half along marked shoulder row and join other shoulder and neckband seams. Cut several 8 cm (3 in) lengths of yarn, then work fringing evenly all round bottom edge as shown in photograph, working a fringe into every stitch, trim neatly to meas 2.5 cm (1 in).

Pin out garment to measurements given and cover with damp cloths and leave to dry naturally. See ball band for washing and further care instructions.

RIT A HAT

SIZES

AGE	0-6 months	6-12 months	1-2 years	2-3 years
Measurement around lower edge				
	34	36	39	43 cm
	13½	14	15½	17 in

YARN

Jody Long Ciao
2 [2: 2: 3] x 50g balls in Poppy 014

NEEDLES

1 pair 3.25 mm (no 10) (US 3) needles
1 pair 4 mm (no 8) (US 6) needles
Cable needle

TENSION

30 sts and 30 rows to 10 cm (4 in) measured over patt using 4 mm (US 6) needles.

ABBREVIATIONS

See inside front flap

SPECIAL ABBREVIATIONS

C2F = slip next st onto cable needle and leave at front of work, K1, then K1 from cable needle.
C4B = slip next 2 sts onto cable needle and leave at back of work, K2, then K2 from cable needle.
C4F = slip next 2 sts onto cable needle and leave at front of work, K2, then K2 from cable needle.

BERET

Using 3.25 mm (US 3) needles cast on 102 [106: 118: 130] sts.
Row 1 (RS): K2, *P2, K2, rep from * to end.
Row 2: P2, *K2, P2, rep from * to end.
These 2 rows form rib.
Work in rib for a further 5 [5: 7: 7] rows, ending with **WS** facing for next row.
Change to 4 mm (US 6) needles.
Next row (WS): P3 [5: 7: 2], (inc **purlwise** into next st, P4 [3: 3: 3], inc **purlwise** into next st, P3 [2: 2: 3]) 11 [14: 15: 16] times, P0 [3: 6: 0]. 124 [134: 148: 162] sts.
Now work in patt as folls:
Row 1 (RS): P2, (K4, P1) 0 [1: 1: 1] times, *K8, P1, K4, P1, rep from * to last 10 [1: 1: 1] sts, K8 [0: 0: 0], P2 [1: 1: 1].
Row 2: K2, (P4, K1) 0 [1: 1: 1] times, *P8, K1, P4, K1, rep from * to last 10 [1: 1: 1] sts, P8 [0: 0: 0], K2 [1: 1: 1].
Row 3: P2, (C4F, P1) 0 [1: 1: 1] times, *C4B, (C4F, P1) twice, rep from * to last 10 [1: 1: 1] sts, (C4B, C4F) 1 [0: 0: 0] times, P2 [1: 1: 1].
Row 4: As row 2.
Row 5: P2, (K4, inc **purlwise** into next st) 0 [1: 1: 1] times, *K8, inc **purlwise** into next st, K4, inc **purlwise** into next st, rep from * to last 10 [15: 15: 15] sts, K8, (inc **purlwise** into next st, K4) 0 [1: 1: 1] times, P2. 140 [152: 168: 184] sts.
Row 6: K2, (P4, K2) 0 [1: 1: 1] times, *P8, K2, P4, K2, rep from * to last 10 [0: 0: 0] sts, (P8, K2) 1 [0: 0: 0] times.
Row 7: P2, (C4F, P2) 0 [1: 1: 1] times, *C4B, (C4F, P2) twice, rep from * to last 10 [0: 0: 0] sts, (C4B, C4F, P2) 1 [0: 0: 0] times.
Row 8: As row 6.
Row 9: P2, (K4, inc **purlwise** into next st, P1) 0 [1: 1: 1] times, *K8, inc **purlwise** into next st, P1, K4, inc **purlwise** into next st, P1, rep from * to last 10 [16: 16: 16] sts, K8, (inc **purlwise** into next st, P1, K4) 0 [1: 1: 1] times, P2. 156 [170: 188: 206] sts.
Row 10: K2, (P4, K3) 0 [1: 1: 1] times, *P8, K3, P4, K3, rep from * to last 10 [17: 17: 17] sts, P8, (K3, P4) 0 [1: 1: 1] times, K2.

Row 11: P2, (C4F, P3) 0 [1: 1: 1] times, *C4B, (C4F, P3) twice, rep from * to last 10 [17: 17: 17] sts, C4B, C4F, (P3, C4F) 0 [1: 1: 1] times, P2.

Row 12: As row 10.

Row 13: P2, (K4, P1, inc **purlwise** into next st, P1) 0 [1: 1: 1] times, *K8, P1, inc **purlwise** into next st, P1, K4, P1, inc **purlwise** into next st, P1, rep from * to last 10 [17: 17: 17] sts, K8, (P1, inc **purlwise** into next st, P1, K4) 0 [1: 1: 1] times, P2. 172 [188: 208: 228]sts.

Row 14: K2, (P4, K4) 0 [1: 1: 1] times, *P8, K4, P4, K4, rep from * to last 10 [18: 18: 18] sts, P8, (K4, P4) 0 [1: 1: 1] times, K2.

Row 15: P2, (C4F, P4) 0 [1: 1: 1] times, *C4B, (C4F, P4) twice, rep from * to last 10 [18: 18: 18] sts, C4B, C4F, (P4, C4F) 0 [1: 1: 1] times, P2.

Row 16: K2, (P4, K4) 0 [1: 1: 1] times, *P8, K4, P4, K4, rep from * to last 10 [18: 18: 18] sts, P8, (K4, P4) 0 [1: 1: 1] times, K2.

Shape Crown

Row 1 (RS): P2 (K4, P1, P2tog, P1) 0 [1: 1: 1] times, *K8, P1, P2tog, P1, K4, P1, P2tog, P1, rep from * to last 10 [18: 18: 18] times, K8, (P1, P2tog, P1, K4) 0 [1: 1: 1] times, P2. 156 [170: 188: 206] sts.

Row 2: K2, (P4, K3) 0 [1: 1: 1] times, *P8, K3, P4, K3, rep from * to last 10 [17: 17: 17] sts, P8, (K3, P4) 0 [1: 1: 1] times, K2.

Row 3: P2, (C4F, P3) 0 [1: 1: 1] times, *C4B, (C4F, P3) twice, rep from * to last 10 [17: 17: 17] sts, C4B, C4F, (P3, C4F) 0 [1: 1: 1] times, P2.

Row 4: As row 2.

Row 5: P2, (K4, P2tog, P1) 0 [1: 1: 1] times, *K8, P2tog, P1, K4, P2tog, P1, rep from * to last 10 [17: 17: 17] sts, K8, (P2tog, P1, K4) 0 [1: 1: 1] times, P2. 140 [152: 168: 184] sts.

Row 6: K2, (P4, K2) 0 [1: 1: 1] times, *P8, K2, P4, K2, rep from * to last 10 [0: 0: 0] sts, (P8, K2) 1 [0: 0: 0] times.

Row 7: P2, (C4F, P2) 0 [1: 1: 1], *C4B, (C4F, P2) twice, rep from * to last 10 [0: 0: 0] sts, (C4B, C4F, P2) 1 [0: 0: 0] times.

Row 8: As row 6.

Row 9: P2, (K4, P2tog) 0 [1: 1: 1] times, *K8, P2tog, K4, P2tog, rep from * to last 10 [16: 16: 16] sts, K8, (P2tog, K4) 0 [1: 1: 1] times, P2. 124 [134: 148: 162] sts.

Row 10: K2, (P4, K1) 0 [1: 1: 1] times, *P8, K1, P4, K1, rep from * to last 10 [1: 1: 1] sts, P8 [0: 0: 0], K2 [1: 1: 1].

Row 11: P2, (C4F, P1) 0 [1: 1: 1] times, *C4B, (C4F, P1) twice, rep from * to last 10 [1: 1: 1] sts, (C4B, C4F) 1 [0: 0: 0] times, P2 [1: 1: 1].

Row 12: As row 10.

Row 13: P2, (K3, sl 1, K1, psso) 0 [1: 1: 1] times, *K8, K2tog, K2, sl 1, K1, psso, rep from * to last 10 [15: 15: 15] sts, K8, (K2tog, K3) 0 [1: 1: 1] times, P2. 108 [116: 128: 140] sts.

Row 14: K2, Purl to last 2 sts, K2.

Row 15: P2, (C4F) 0 [1: 1: 1] times, *C4B, (C4F) twice, rep from * to last 10 [2: 2: 2] sts, (C4B, C4F) 1 [0: 0: 0] times, P2.

Row 16: As row 14.

Row 17: P2, (sl 1, K1, psso, K2tog) 0 [1: 1: 1] times, *K8, sl 1, K1, psso, K2tog, rep from * to last 10 [2: 2: 2] sts, K8 [0: 0: 0], P2. 92 [96: 106: 116] sts.

Row 18: As row 14.

Row 19: P2, (C2F) 0 [1: 1: 1] times, *C4B, C4F, C2F, rep from * to last 10 [2: 2: 2] sts, (C4B, C4F) 1 [0: 0: 0] times, P2.

Row 20: As row 14.

Row 21: P2, (sl 1, K1, psso) 0 [1: 1: 1] times, *K8, sl 1, K1, psso, rep from * to last 10 [2: 2: 2] sts, K8 [0: 0: 0], P2. 84 [86: 95: 104] sts.

Row 22: As row 14.

Row 23: P2, K0 [1: 1: 1], *C4B, C4F, K1, rep from * to last 10 [2: 2: 2] sts, (C4B, C4F) 1 [0: 0: 0] times, P2.

Row 24: As row 14.

Row 25: P2, K0 [1: 1: 1], *K2tog, K5, sl 1, K1, psso, rep from * to last 10 [2: 2: 2] sts, (sl 1, K1, psso, K4, K2tog) 1 [0: 0: 0] times, P2. 66 [68: 75: 82] sts.

Row 26: As row 14.

Row 27: P2, K0 [1: 1: 1], *K2tog, K3, sl 1, K1, psso, rep from * to last 8 [2: 2: 2] sts, (K2tog, K2, sl 1, K1, psso) 1 [0: 0: 0] times, P2. 48 [50: 55: 60] sts.

Row 28: K2, (P2tog tbl, P2tog) 1 [0: 0: 0] times, *P2tog tbl, P1, P2tog, rep from * to last 2 [3: 3: 3] sts, P0 [1: 1: 1], K2. 30 [32: 35: 38] sts.

Row 29: P2tog, K0 [0: 1: 0], (K2tog) 13 [14: 15: 17] times, P2tog. Break off yarn, thread through rem 15 [16: 18: 19] sts, pull up tightly and fasten off securely.

MAKING UP

Join centre back seam of Beret by joining row-ends together. Cover with damp cloths and leave to dry naturally. See ball band for washing and further care instructions.

SKILL LEVEL

RIZZO

SIZES

AGE	0-6 months	6-12 months	1-2 years	2-3 years
To fit chest				
	41	46	51	56 cm
	16	18	20	22 in
Actual chest measurement				
	46	52	57	63 cm
	18	20½	22½	24¾ in
Full length, from shoulder				
	24	28	32	38 cm
	9½	11	12½	15 in
Sleeve length				
	15	17	20	24 cm
	6	6½	8	9½ in

YARN
Jody Long Ciao
A 3 [3: 4: 5] x 50g balls in Avocado 011
B 1 [1: 1: 1] x 50g ball in Cocoa 005
C 1 [1: 1: 1] x 50g ball in Petal 020
D 1 [1: 1: 1] x 50g ball in Pitch 001
E 1 [1: 1: 1] x 50g ball in Dijon 016
F 1 [1: 1: 1] x 50g ball in Alabaster 002
G 1 [1: 1: 1] x 50g ball in Myrtle 010

NEEDLES
1 pair 3.25 mm (no 10) (US 3) needles
1 pair 4 mm (no 8) (US 6) needles

BUTTONS - 2 [2: 0: 0]

TENSION
22 sts and 30 rows to 10 cm (4 in) measured over st st using 4 mm (US 6) needles.

ABBREVIATIONS
See inside front flap

CHART NOTE
Chart is worked in st st – work odd numbered rows as RS (K) rows and even numbered rows as WS (P) rows. Use a separate ball of yarn for each block of colour, twisting yarns tog on WS where they meet (to avoid holes forming).

BACK
Using 3.25 mm (US 3) needles and yarn **A** cast on 51 [57: 63: 69] sts.
Work in g st for 6 [6: 8: 8] rows, ending with RS facing for next row.
Change to 4 mm (US 6) needles.
Beg with a K row, now work in st st throughout as folls:
**Cont straight until Back meas 14 [17: 20: 25] cm (5½ [6¾: 8: 9¾] in), ending with RS facing for next row.

Shape Armholes
Cast off 3 sts at beg of next 2 rows. 45 [51: 57: 63] sts.
Dec 1 st at each end of next 1 [3: 3: 5] rows, then on foll 3 [2: 3: 2] alt rows. 37 [41: 45: 49] sts.**
Cont straight until armhole meas 10 [11: 12: 13] cm (4 [4¼: 4¾: 5] in), ending with RS facing for next row.

Shape Shoulders
Cast off 4 [4: 5: 5] sts at beg of next 2 rows, then 4 [5: 5: 6] sts at beg of foll 2 rows.
Break yarn and leave rem 21 [23: 25: 27] sts on a holder (for Neckband).

FRONT

Using 3.25 mm (US 3) needles and yarn **A** cast on 51 [57: 63: 69] sts.

Work in g st for 6 [6: 8: 8] rows, ending with RS facing for next row.

Change to 4 mm (US 6) needles.

Now place chart (see chart note) as folls:

Next row (RS): Using yarn **A** K4 [7: 10: 13], work next 43 sts as row 1 of chart, using yarn **A** K4 [7: 10: 13].

Next row: Using yarn **A** P4 [7: 10: 13], work next 43 sts as row 2 of chart, using yarn **A** P4 [7: 10: 13].

These 2 rows set the sts – chart worked over central 43 sts and side sts worked in st st using yarn **A**.

Keeping sts correct as now set, cont as folls:

(**Note:** Once all 46 rows of chart have been completed, complete Front in st st using yarn **A only**.)

Work as given for Back from ** to **.

Cont straight until 12 [14: 16: 16] rows less have been worked than on Back to beg of shoulder shaping, ending with RS facing for next row.

Shape Front Neck

Next row (RS): K14 [16: 18: 19] and turn, leaving rem sts on a holder.

Dec 1 st at neck edge of next 4 rows, then on foll 2 [3: 4: 4] alt rows. 8 [9: 10: 11] sts.

Work 1 [1: 3: 3] rows, ending with RS facing for next row.

(**Note:** For 1st and 2nd sizes, this shoulder edge is 2 rows lower than right shoulder as the buttonhole border will be added.)

Shape Shoulder

Cast off 4 [4: 5: 5] sts at beg of next row.

Work 1 row.

Cast off rem 4 [5: 5: 6] sts.

Return to sts on holder and slip central 9 [9: 9: 11] sts onto another holder (for Neckband). Rejoin yarn to rem sts and K to end. 14 [16: 18: 19] sts.

Dec 1 st at neck edge of next 4 rows, then on foll 2 [3: 4: 4] alt rows. 8 [9: 10: 11] sts.

Work 4 rows, ending with **WS** facing for next row.

Shape Shoulder

Cast off 4 [4: 5: 5] sts at beg of next row.

Work 1 row.

Cast off rem 4 [5: 5: 6] sts.

SLEEVES

Using 3.25 mm (US 3) needles and yarn **A** cast on 27 [29: 31: 33] sts.

Work in g st for 6 [6: 8: 8] rows, ending with RS facing for next row.

Change to 4 mm (US 6) needles.

Beg with a K row, now work in st st throughout as folls:

Inc 1 st at each end of next [3rd: 3rd: 3rd] and every foll 4th row to 43 [47: 51: 47] sts, then on 0 [0: 0: 4] foll 6th rows. 43 [47: 51: 55] sts.

Cont straight until Sleeve meas 15 [17: 20: 24] cm (6 [6¾: 8: 9½] in), ending with RS facing for next row.

Shape Top

Cast off 3 sts at beg of next 2 rows. 37 [41: 45: 49] sts.

Dec 1 st at each end of next 3 rows, then on foll 4 [5: 6: 7] alt rows, then on foll 5 rows, ending with RS facing for next row.

Cast off rem 13 [15: 17: 19] sts.

MAKING UP

Join right shoulder seam.

Neckband

With RS facing, using 3.25 mm (US 3) needles and yarn **A**, pick up and knit 9 [11: 15: 17] sts down left side of front neck, K across 9 [9: 9: 11] sts on front holder, pick up and knit 11 [13: 15: 17] sts up right side of front neck, then K across 21 [23: 25: 27] sts on back holder. 50 [56: 64: 72] sts.

Work in g st for 4 [4: 6: 6] rows, ending with **WS** facing for next row.

Cast off **knitwise** (on **WS**).

For 1st and 2nd Sizes Only
Back Button Border

With RS facing, using 3.25 mm (US 3) needles and yarn A, pick up

and knit 12 [13] sts evenly across left back shoulder edge, from top of neckband to armhole edge.

Work in g st for 4 rows, ending with **WS** facing for next row.

Cast off **knitwise** (on **WS**).

Front Buttonhole Border

With RS facing, using 3.25 mm (US 3) needles and yarn A, pick up and knit 12 [13] sts evenly across left front shoulder edge, from armhole edge to top of neckband.

Row 1 (WS): Knit.

Row 2: K4, yo, K2tog (to make first buttonhole), K3 [4], yo, K2tog (to make 2nd buttonhole), K1.

Work in g st for a further 2 rows, ending with **WS** facing for next row.

Cast off **knitwise** (on **WS**).

Lay Front Buttonhole Border over Back Button Border so that borders overlap. Sew together at armhole edge. Attach buttons to correspond with buttonholes.

For 3rd and 4th Sizes only

Join left shoulder and neckband seam.

For All Sizes

Join side seams. Join sleeve seams. Insert sleeves into armholes. Pin out garment to measurements given, cover with damp cloths and leave to dry naturally. See ball band for washing and further care instructions.

Key ▨ A ▨ B ☐ C ■ D ▨ E ☐ F ▨ G

SKILL LEVEL

ROME

SIZES

AGE	0-6 months	6-12 months	1-2 years	2-3 years
To fit chest				
	41	46	51	56 cm
	16	18	20	22 in
Actual chest measurement				
	45	50	55	61 cm
	17¾	19¾	21¾	24 in
Full length, from shoulder				
	24	28	32	38 cm
	9½	11	12½	15 in
Sleeve length				
	15	17	20	24 cm
	6	6½	8	9½ in

YARN
Jody Long Ciao

Boys Version
A 1 [2: 2: 3] x 50g balls in Cocoa 005
B 1 [2: 2: 2] x 50g balls in Myrtle 010
C 1 [1: 2: 2] x 50g balls in Marigold 015

Girls Version
A 1 [2: 2: 3] x 50g balls in Boysenberry 017
B 1 [2: 2: 2] x 50g balls in Fuchsia 019
C 1 [1: 2: 2] x 50g balls in Myrtle 010

NEEDLES
1 pair 3.25 mm (no 10) (US 3) needles
1 pair 4 mm (no 8) (US 6) needles

TENSION
22 sts and 30 rows to 10 cm (4 in) measured over st st using 4 mm (US 6) needles.

ABBREVIATIONS
See inside front flap

BACK
Using 3.25 mm (US 3) needles and yarn **A** cast on 49 [55: 61: 67] sts.
Work in g st for 2 [2: 4: 4] rows, ending with RS facing for next row.
Change to 4 mm (US 6) needles.
Beg with a K row, work in striped st st as folls:
Using yarn **B**, work 6 rows.
Using yarn **C**, work 6 rows.
Using yarn **A**, work 6 rows.
These 18 rows form striped st st.
Cont in striped st st until Back meas 23 [27: 31: 37] cm
(9 [10½: 12¼: 14½] in), ending with RS facing for next row.

Shape Back Neck
Keeping stripes correct, work as folls:
Next row (RS): K17 [19: 22: 23] and turn, leaving rem sts on a holder.
Next row: Cast off 2 [2: 2: 4] sts, P to end. 15 [17: 20: 19] sts. Place a marker at end of last row to mark shoulder position.

Shape Shoulder
Keeping stripes correct, dec 1 st at neck edge of next and foll 3 alt rows, ending with **WS** facing for next row. 11 [13: 16: 15] sts.
Cast off 5 [3: 4: 4] sts, P to end. 6 [10: 12: 11] sts.
Work 1 row.

0-6 Months Only
Cast off rem 6 sts.

6-12 Months, 1-2 Years and 2-3 Years Only
Cast off [4: 5: 5] sts, P to end. [6: 7: 6] sts.
Work 1 row.
Cast off rem [6: 7: 6] sts.

All Sizes
Return to sts on holder and slip central 15 [17: 17: 21] sts onto another holder (for Back Shoulder and Neck Border). Rejoin appropriate yarn to rem sts and keeping stripes correct, work as folls:
Next row (RS): Cast off 2 [2: 2: 4] sts, K to end. 15 [17: 20: 19] sts.
Work 1 row, ending with RS facing for next row. Place a marker at beg of last row to mark shoulder position.

Shape Shoulder
Keeping stripes correct, dec 1 st at neck edge of next and foll 3 alt rows, ending with **WS** facing for next row. 11 [13: 16: 15] sts.
Work 1 row.
Cast off 5 [3: 4: 4] sts, K to end. 6 [10: 12: 11] sts.
Work 1 row.

0-6 Months Only
Cast off rem 6 sts.

6-12 Months, 1-2 Years and 2-3 Years Only
Cast off [4: 5: 5] sts, K to end. [6: 7: 6] sts.
Work 1 row.
Cast off rem [6: 7: 6] sts.

FRONT
Work as given for Back until 4 [4: 4: 6] rows less have been worked than on Back to beg of back neck shaping, ending with RS facing for next row.

Shape Front Neck
Next row (RS): K17 [19: 20: 23] and turn, leaving rem sts on a holder.
Next row: Purl.
Keeping stripes correct, dec 1 st at neck edge of next 2 [2: 2: 4] rows, ending with RS facing for next row. 15 [17: 18: 19] sts. Place a marker at end of last row for shoulder position.

Shape Shoulder
Keeping stripes correct, dec 1 st at neck edge of next and foll 3 alt rows, ending with **WS** facing for next row. 11 [13: 14: 15] sts.
Next row (WS): Cast off 5 [3: 3: 4] sts, P to end. 6 [10: 11: 11] sts.
Work 1 row.

0-6 Months Only
Cast off rem 6 sts.

6-12 Months, 1-2 Years and 2-3 Years Only
Cast off [4: 4: 5] sts, P to end. [6: 7: 6] sts.
Work 1 row.
Cast off rem [6: 7: 6] sts.

All Sizes
Return to sts on holder and slip central 15 [17: 21: 21] sts onto another holder (for Front Shoulder and Neck Border). Rejoin appropriate yarn to rem sts and keeping stripes correct, K to end. 17 [19: 20: 23] sts.
Work 1 row, ending with RS facing for next row.
Keeping stripes correct, dec 1 st at neck edge of next 2 [2: 2: 4] rows, ending with RS facing for next row. 15 [17: 18: 19] sts. Place a marker at beg of last row for shoulder position.

Shape Shoulder
Keeping stripes correct, dec 1 st at neck edge of next and foll 3 alt rows, ending with **WS** facing for next row. 11 [13: 14: 15] sts.
Work 1 row.
Next row (RS): Cast off 5 [3: 3: 4] sts, K to end. 6 [10: 11: 11] sts.
Work 1 row.

0-6 Months Only
Cast off rem 6 sts.

6-12 Months, 1-2 Years and 2-3 Years Only
Cast off [4: 4: 5] sts, K to end. [6: 7: 6] sts.
Work 1 row.
Cast off rem [6: 7: 6] sts.

SLEEVES
Using 3.25 mm (US 3) needles and yarn **A** cast on 29 [31: 33: 35] sts.
Work in g st for 2 [2: 4: 4] rows, ending with RS facing for next row.
Change to 4 mm (US 6) needles.
Beg with a K row, work in striped st st as given for Back as folls:

Inc 1 st at each end of next [3rd: 3rd: 3rd] and every foll 4th row to 43 [47: 51: 47] sts, then on 0 [0: 0: 4] foll 6th rows. 43 [47: 51: 55] sts. Cont straight until Sleeve meas 15 [17: 20: 24] cm (6 [6¾: 8: 9½] in), ending with RS facing for next row.

Shape Top

Keeping stripes correct, cast off 6 [6: 7: 8] sts at beg of next 2 [6: 4: 2] rows, then 5 [0: 6: 7] sts at beg of foll 4 [0: 2: 4] rows.
Cast off rem 11 sts.

MAKING UP

Join right shoulder seam.

Back Shoulder and Neck Border

With RS facing, using 3.25 mm (US 3) needles and yarn **A**, pick up and knit 22 [25: 27: 28] sts across shoulder and down right side of back neck, K across 15 [17: 17: 21] sts on back holder, pick up and knit 22 [25: 27: 28] sts up left side of back neck and across shoulder. 59 [67: 71: 77] sts.
Work in g st for 2 rows, ending with **WS** facing for next row.
Cast off **knitwise** (on **WS**).

Front Shoulder and Neck Border

With RS facing, using 3.25 mm (US 3) needles and yarn **A**, pick up and knit 23 [26: 28: 29] sts across shoulder and down right side of back neck, K across 15 [17: 21: 21] sts on front holder, pick up and knit 23 [26: 28: 29] sts up left side of front neck and across shoulder. 61 [69: 77: 79] sts.
Work in g st for 2 rows, ending with **WS** facing for next row.
Cast off **knitwise** (on **WS**).

Place back shoulder and neck border over front shoulder and neck border matching markers and sew together at side edges (do not remove markers - Markers now become shoulder seam). Mark points along side seam edges 10 [11: 12: 13] cm (4 [4¼: 4¾: 5] in) either side of shoulder seams (original markers), then sew shaped cast-off edge of sleeve to back and front between these points. Join side and sleeve seams.

Pin out garment to measurements given, cover with damp cloths and leave to dry naturally. See ball band for washing and further care instructions.

SKILL LEVEL

ROSA

SIZES

AGE	0-6 months	6-12 months	1-2 years	2-3 years
To fit chest				
	41	46	51	56 cm
	16	18	20	22 in
Actual chest measurement				
	46	52	57	63 cm
	18	20½	22½	24¾ in
Full length, from shoulder				
	24	28	32	38 cm
	9½	11	12½	15 in
Sleeve length				
	15	17	20	24 cm
	6	6½	8	9½ in

YARN

Jody Long Ciao
A 3 [4: 4: 5] x 50g balls in Alabaster 002
B 1 [1: 1: 1] x 50g balls in Avocado 011
C 1 [1: 1: 1] x 50g balls in Fuchsia 019
D 1 [1: 1: 1] x 50g balls in Petal 020

NEEDLES

1 pair 3.25 mm (no 10) (US 3) needles
1 pair 4 mm (no 8) (US 6) needles

BUTTONS - 5 [5: 6: 6]

TENSION

22 sts and 30 rows to 10 cm (4 in) measured over patt using 4 mm (US 6) needles.

ABBREVIATIONS

See inside front flap

Pattern note: The cardigan was designed with the intarsia method in mind, although you may wish to knit all the cardigan pieces in yarn **A** throughout then use Swiss (duplicate) stitch for the flower motifs before seaming the pieces together.

BACK

Using 3.25 mm (US 3) needles and yarn **A** cast on 51 [57: 63: 69] sts.
Work in g st for 6 [6: 8: 8] rows, ending with RS facing for next row.
Change to 4 mm (US 6) needles.
Beg and ending rows as indicated, and repeating the 20 row patt rep throughout, and using a separate ball of yarn for each block of colour, twisting yarns together on WS where they meet to avoid holes forming, cont in patt from chart which is worked entirely in st st beg with a K row.
Cont in patt until Back meas 14 [17: 20: 25] cm (5½ [6½: 8: 9¾] in), ending with RS facing for next row.

Shape Armholes

Keeping patt correct, cast off 3 sts at beg of next 2 rows.
45 [51: 57: 63] sts.
Dec 1 st at each end of next 1 [3: 3: 5] rows, then on foll 3 [2: 3: 2] alt rows. 37 [41: 45: 49] sts.
Cont straight until armhole meas 10 [11: 12: 13] cm (4 [4¼: 4¾: 5] in), ending with RS facing for next row.

Shape Shoulders

Keeping patt correct, cast off 4 [5: 5: 6] sts at beg of next 2 rows, then 5 [5: 6: 6] sts at beg of foll 2 rows.
Break yarn and leave rem 19 [21: 23: 25] sts on a holder (for Neckband).

LEFT FRONT

Using 3.25 mm (US 3) needles and yarn **A** cast on 25 [28: 31: 34] sts.

Work in g st for 6 [6: 8: 8] rows, ending with RS facing for next row. Change to 4 mm (US 6) needles.

Beg and ending rows as indicated, omitting part motifs at centre front and repeating the 20 row patt rep throughout, cont in patt until Left Front matches Back to beg of armhole shaping, ending with RS facing for next row.

Shape Armhole

Keeping patt correct, cast off 3 sts at beg of next row. 22 [25: 28: 31] sts.

Work 1 row.

Dec 1 st at armhole edge of next 1 [3: 3: 5] rows, then on foll 3 [2: 3: 2] alt rows. 18 [20: 22: 24] sts.

Cont straight until 12 [14: 16: 16] rows less have been worked than on Back to beg of shoulder shaping, ending with RS facing for next row.

Shape Front Neck

Next row (RS): Patt 15 [17: 19: 20] sts and turn, leaving rem 3 [3: 3: 4] sts on a holder (for Neckband).

Keeping patt correct, dec 1 st at neck edge of next 4 rows, then on foll 2 [3: 4: 4] alt rows. 9 [10: 11: 12] sts.

Work 3 rows, ending with RS facing for next row.

Shape Shoulders

Keeping patt correct, cast off 4 [5: 5: 6] sts at beg of next row.

Work 1 row.

Cast off rem 5 [5: 6: 6] sts.

RIGHT FRONT

Using 3.25 mm (US 3) needles and yarn **A** cast on 25 [28: 31: 34] sts.

Work in g st for 6 [6: 8: 8] rows, ending with RS facing for next row. Change to 4 mm (US 6) needles.

Beg and ending rows as indicated, omitting part motifs at centre front and repeating the 20 row patt rep throughout, cont in patt until Right Front matches Back to beg of armhole shaping, ending with RS facing for next row.

Shape Armhole

Work 1 row.

Keeping patt correct, cast off 3 sts at beg of next row. 22 [25: 28: 31] sts.

Dec 1 st at armhole edge of next 1 [3: 3: 5] rows, then on foll 3 [2: 3: 2] alt rows. 18 [20: 22: 24] sts.

Cont straight until 12 [14: 16: 16] rows less have been worked than on Back to beg of shoulder shaping, ending with RS facing for next row.

Shape Front Neck

Next row (RS): K3 [3: 3: 4] and slip these sts onto a holder (for Neckband), patt to end. 15 [17: 19: 20] sts.

Keeping patt correct, dec 1 st at neck edge of next 4 rows, then on foll 2 [3: 4: 4] alt rows. 9 [10: 11: 12] sts.

Work 4 rows, ending with **WS** facing for next row.

Shape Shoulders

Keeping patt correct, cast off 4 [5: 5: 6] sts at beg of next row.

Work 1 row.

Cast off rem 5 [5: 6: 6] sts.

SLEEVES

Using 3.25 mm (US 3) needles and yarn **A** cast on 27 [29: 31: 33] sts.

Work in g st for 6 [6: 8: 8] rows, ending with RS facing for next row.

Change to 4 mm (US 6) needles.

Beg and ending rows as indicated, and repeating the 20 row patt rep throughout, cont in patt from chart, shaping sides by inc 1 st at each end of next [3rd: 3rd: 3rd] and every foll 4th row until there are 43 [47: 51: 47] sts, then on 0 [0: 0: 4] foll 6th rows. 43 [47: 51: 55] sts.

Cont straight until Sleeve meas 15 [17: 20: 24] cm (6 [6¾: 8: 9½] in), ending with RS facing for next row.

Shape Top

Keeping patt correct, cast off 3 sts at beg of next 2 rows. 37 [41: 45: 49] sts.

Dec 1 st at each end of next 3 rows, then on foll 4 alt rows, then on every row until 13 sts rem, ending with RS facing for next row.

Cast off rem 13 sts.

MAKING UP

Join both shoulder seams.

Neckband

With RS facing, using 3.25 mm (US 3) needles and yarn **A**, slip 3 [3: 3: 4] sts on right front holder onto right needle, rejoin yarn and pick up and knit 11 [13: 15: 15] sts up right side of front neck, K across 19 [21: 23: 25] sts on back holder, pick up and knit 11 [13: 15: 15] sts down left side of front neck, then K across 3 [3: 3: 4] sts on left front holder. 47 [53: 59: 63] sts.

Work in g st for 4 [4: 6: 6] rows, ending with **WS** facing for next row.

Cast off in **knitwise** (on **WS**).

Button Band

With RS facing, using 3.25 mm (US 3) needles and yarn **A**, pick up and knit 53 [61: 71: 85] sts evenly down entire left front opening edge, from top of Neckband to cast-on edge.

Work in g st for 6 rows, ending with **WS** facing for next row.

Cast off in **knitwise** (on **WS**).

Buttonhole Band

With RS facing, using 3.25 mm (US 3) needles and yarn A, pick up and knit 53 [61: 71: 85] sts evenly up entire right front opening edge, from cast-on edge to top of Neckband.

Work in g st for 3 rows, ending with RS facing for next row.

Row 4 (RS): K1 [1: 2: 1], *K2tog, yo (to make a buttonhole), K10 [12: 11: 14], rep from * 3 [3: 4: 4] times more, K2tog, yo (to make 5th [5th: 6th: 6th] buttonhole), K2.

Work in g st for a further 2 rows, ending with WS facing for next row.

Cast off in **knitwise** (on **WS**).

Join side seams. Join sleeve seams. Sew sleeves into armholes. Sew on buttons.

Pin out garment to measurements given and cover with damp cloths and leave to dry naturally. See ball band for washing and further care instructions.

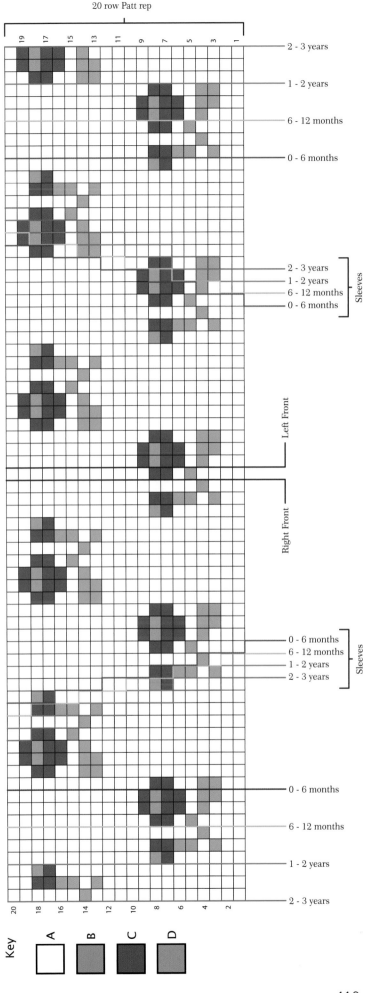

SKILL LEVEL

SCILLY

SIZES

AGE	0-6 months	6-12 months	1-2 years	2-3 years
To fit chest				
	41	46	51	56 cm
	16	18	20	22 in
Actual chest measurement				
	45	51	56	62 cm
	17¾	20	22	24¼ in
Full length, from back neck				
	24	28	32	38 cm
	9½	11	12½	15 in
Sleeve length				
	15	17	20	24 cm
	6	6½	8	9½ in

YARN
Jody Long Ciao
A 2 [3: 3: 4] x 50g balls in Avocado 011
B 1 [2: 2: 2] x 50g balls in Boysenberry 017

NEEDLES
1 pair 3.25 mm (no 10) (US 3) needles
1 pair 4 mm (no 8) (US 6) needles

BUTTONS - 5 [5: 5: 6]

TENSION
22 sts and 30 rows to 10 cm (4 in) measured over striped st st using 4 mm (US 6) needles.

ABBREVIATIONS
See inside front flap

BACK
Using 3.25 mm (US 3) needles and yarn **A** cast on 58 [66: 70: 78] sts.
Row 1 (RS): *K2, P2, rep from * to last 2 sts, K2.
Row 2: *P2, K2, rep from * to last 2 sts, P2.
These 2 rows form rib.
Cont in rib for a further 7 [7: 9: 9] rows, ending with **WS** facing for next row.
Next row (WS): P4 [5: 6: 2], P2tog, (P5 [4: 6: 6], P2tog), 7 [9: 7: 9] times, P3 [5: 6: 2]. 50 [56: 62: 68] sts.
Change to 4 mm (US 6) needles.
Beg with a K row, now work in striped st st as folls:
Using yarn **B**, work 4 rows.
Using yarn **A**, work 4 rows.
These 8 rows form striped st st.
Cont in striped st st until Back meas 12 [15: 18: 23] cm (4¾ [6: 7: 9] in), ending with RS facing for next row.

Shape Raglan Armholes
Keeping stripes correct, cast off 3 [3: 3: 4] sts at beg of next 2 rows. 44 [50: 56: 60] sts.

1-2 and 2-3 Years Only
Next row (RS): K1, sl 1, K1, psso, K to last 3 sts, K2tog, K1.
Next row: P1, P2tog, P to last 2 sts, P2tog tbl, P1.
Rep the last 2 rows [0: 1] time more. [52: 52] sts.

For All Sizes
Next row (RS): K1, sl 1, K1, psso, K to last 3 sts, K2tog, K1.
Next row: Purl.
These 2 rows set raglan armhole shaping.
Dec 1 st at each end as before on next and foll 11 [13: 13: 13] alt rows. 18 [20: 22: 22] sts.
Work 1 row, ending with RS facing for next row.
Cast off.

LEFT FRONT

Using 3.25 mm (US 3) needles and yarn **A** cast on 27 [31: 35: 35] sts.

Row 1 (RS): *K2, P2, rep from * to last 3 sts, K3.

Row 2: K1, P2, *K2, P2 rep from * to end.

These 2 rows form rib.

Cont in rib for a further 7 [7: 9: 9] rows, ending with **WS** facing for next row.

Next row (WS): P4 [2: 1: 4], P2tog, (P4 [3: 3: 6], P2tog) 3 [5: 6: 3] times, P3 [2: 2: 5]. 23 [25: 28: 31] sts.

Change to 4 mm (US 6) needles.

Beg with a K row, work in striped st st as given for Back as folls:
Cont straight until Left Front matches Back to beg of raglan armhole shaping, ending with RS facing for next row and ending on the same stripe as Back to start of raglan shaping.

Shape Raglan Armhole

Keeping stripes correct, cast off 3 [3: 3: 4] sts at beg of next row. 20 [22: 25: 27] sts.

Work 1 row, ending with RS facing for next row.

1-2 and 2-3 Years Only

Next row (RS): K1, sl 1, K1, psso, K to end.

Next row: P to last 3 sts, P2tog tbl, P1.

Rep the last 2 rows [0: 1] time more. [23: 23] sts.

For All Sizes

Next row (RS): K1, sl 1, K1, psso, K to end.

Next row: Purl.

These 2 rows set raglan armhole shaping.

Dec 1 st at raglan edge as before on next and foll 10 [12: 12: 11] alt rows, and ending with **WS** facing for next row. 8 [8: 9: 10] sts.

Shape Neck

Keeping patt correct, cast off 4 [4: 5: 4] sts at beg of next row. 4 [4: 4: 6] sts.

0-6 Months, 6-12 Months and 1-2 Years Only

Next row (RS): K1, sl 1, K2tog, psso. 2 [2: 2] sts.

2-3 Years Only

Next row (RS): K1, sl 1, K1, psso, K1, K2tog. 4 sts.

Next row: P2tog, P2. 3 sts.

Next row: K1, sl 1, K1, psso. 2 sts.

For All Sizes

Next row (WS): P2tog. Fasten off.

RIGHT FRONT

Using 3.25 mm (US 3) needles and yarn **A** cast on 27 [31: 35: 35] sts.

Row 1 (RS): K1, *K2, P2, rep from * to last 2 sts, K2.

Row 2: *P2, K2, rep from * to last 3 sts, P2, K1.

These 2 rows form rib.

Cont in rib for a further 7 [7: 9: 9] rows, ending with **WS** facing for next row.

Next row (WS): P3 [2: 2: 5], P2tog, (P4 [3: 3: 6], P2tog) 3 [5: 6: 3] times, P4 [2: 1: 4]. 23 [25: 28: 31] sts.

Change to 4 mm (US 6) needles.

Beg with a K row, work in striped st st as given for Back as folls:
Cont straight until Right Front matches Back to beg of raglan armhole shaping, ending with **WS** facing for next row and ending on the same stripe as Back to start of raglan shaping.

Shape Raglan Armhole

Keeping stripes correct, cast off 3 [3: 3: 4] sts at beg of next row. 20 [22: 25: 27] sts.

1-2 and 2-3 Years Only

Next row (RS): K to last 3 sts, K2tog, K1.

Next row: P1, P2tog, P to end.

Rep the last 2 rows [0: 1] time more. [23: 23] sts.

For All Sizes

Next row (RS): K to last 3 sts, K2tog, K1.

Next row: Purl.

These 2 rows set raglan armhole shaping.

Dec 1 st at raglan edge as before on next and foll 9 [11: 11: 10] alt rows. 9 [9: 10: 11] sts.

Work 1 row, ending with RS facing for next row.

Shape Neck

Keeping patt correct work as folls:

Next row (RS): Cast off 4 [4: 5: 4] sts, K to last 3 sts, K2tog, K1. 4 [4: 4: 6] sts.

Work 1 row, ending with RS facing for next row.

0-6 Months, 6-12 Months and 1-2 Years Only

Next row (RS): Sl 1, K2tog, psso, K1. 2 [2: 2] sts.

2-3 Years Only

Next row (RS): (K2tog, K1) twice. 4 sts.

Next row: P2, P2tog. 3 sts.

Next row: K2tog, K1. 2 sts.

For All Sizes

Next row (WS): P2tog. Fasten off.

SLEEVES

Using 3.25 mm (US 3) needles and yarn **A** cast on 42 [42: 46: 46] sts.

Work in rib as given for Back for 9 [9: 11: 11] rows, ending with **WS** facing for next row.

Next row (WS): P3 [3: 1: 2], P2tog, (P5 [5: 4: 6], P2tog) 5 [5: 7: 5] times, P2 [2: 1: 2]. 36 [36: 38: 40] sts.

Change to 4 mm (US 6) needles.

Beg with a K row, work in striped st st as given for Back as folls:
Work 12 [4: 4: 4] rows, ending with RS facing for next row.

Next row (RS): K2, M1, K to last 2 sts, M1, K2. 38 [38: 40: 42] sts.

Keeping stripes correct and working all increases as set by last row, inc 1 st at each end of every foll 12th [8th: 8th: 8th] row to 40 [44: 48: 48] sts, then on every foll - [-: -: 10th] row until there are - [-: -: 52] sts.

Cont straight until Sleeve meas approx 15 [17: 20: 24] cm (6 [6½: 8: 9½] in), ending with RS facing for next row and ending on the same stripe as Back to start of raglan shaping.

Shape Raglan

Keeping stripes correct, cast off 3 [3: 3: 4] sts at beg of next 2 rows. 34 [38: 42: 44] sts.

Working all decreases as set by back raglan, dec 1 st at each end of next and foll 4th row, then on foll 9 [11: 12: 13] alt rows. 12 [12: 14: 14] sts.

Work 1 row, ending with RS facing for next row.

Cast off.

MAKING UP

Join raglan seams.

Left Front border

With RS facing using 3.25 mm (US 3) needles and yarn **A** pick up and knit 56 [68: 80: 88] sts evenly down left front opening edge, from start of neck shaping to cast-on edge.

Row 1 (WS): K1, *P2, K2, rep from * to last 3 sts, P2, K1.

Row 2: K3, *P2, K2, rep from * to last st, K1.

These 2 rows for rib.

Work in rib for a further 2 rows, ending with **WS** facing for next row.

For a Girl

Work in rib for a further 5 rows, ending with RS facing for next row.

Cast off in rib.

For a Boy

Row 5 (WS): Rib 3, *yo, work 2 tog (to make a buttonhole), rib 10 [13: 16: 14], rep from * 3 [3: 3: 4] times more, yo, work 2 tog (to make 5th [5th: 5th: 6th] buttonhole), rib 3.

Work in rib for a further 4 rows, ending with RS facing for next row. Cast off in rib.

Right Front border

With RS facing using 3.25 mm (US 3) needles and yarn **A** pick up and knit 56 [68: 80: 88] sts evenly down right front opening edge, from cast-on edge to start of neck shaping.

Beg with row 1, work in rib as given for Button Band for 4 rows, ending with **WS** facing for next row.

For a Girl

Row 5 (WS): Rib 3, *yo, work 2 tog (to make a buttonhole), rib 10 [13: 16: 14], rep from * 3 [3: 3: 4] times more, yo, work 2 tog (to make 5th [5th: 5th: 6th] buttonhole), rib 3.

Work a further 4 rows in rib, ending with RS facing or next row. Cast off in rib.

For a Boy

Work in rib for a further 5 rows, ending with RS facing for next row. Cast off in rib.

Collar

Join raglan seams.

With RS facing using 3.25 mm (US 3) needles and yarn **A**, starting halfway across top of right front border, pick up and knit 10 [11: 10: 12] sts evenly up right side of neck, 12 [14: 14: 14] sts from 12 [12: 14: 14] cast off sts at top of right sleeve, 21 [23: 26: 25] sts from 18 [20: 22: 22] cast off sts at back of neck, 12 [14: 14: 14] sts from 12 [12: 14: 14] cast off sts at top of left sleeve, 10 [11: 10: 12] sts evenly down left side of neck, ending halfway across top of left front border. 65 [73: 74: 77] sts.

Row 1: K3, (P2, K2) 5 [6: 5: 5] times, (P1, K2) 7 [7: 10: 11] times, (P2, K2) 5 [6: 5: 5] times, K1.

Row 2: K1, (P2, K2) 5 [6: 5: 5] times, (P2, K1) 7 [7: 10: 11] times, (P2, K2) 5 [6: 5: 5] times, P2, K1.

Row 3: As row 1.

Row 4: K1, (P2, K2) 5 [6: 5: 5] times, (P2, inc knitwise into next st) 7 [7: 10: 11] times, (P2, K2) 5 [6: 5: 5] times, P2, K1.

Row 5: K1, *K2, P2, rep from * to last 3 sts, K3.

Row 6: K1, *P2, K2, rep from * to last 3 sts, P2, K1.

Rep the last 2 rows until Collar meas 7 [7: 8: 8] cm (2¾ [2¾: 3: 3] in), ending with a 5th row.

Next row: K1, (P2, K2) 4 [5: 4: 4] times, (P2, inc knitwise into next st, K1) 9 [9: 12: 13] times, (P2, K2) 4 [5: 4: 4] times, P2, K1. 81 [89: 96: 101] sts.

Cast off in patt.

Join side and sleeve seams. Sew on buttons.

Pin out garment to measurements given and cover with damp cloths and leave to dry naturally. See ball band for washing and further care instructions.

SIENNA

SIZES

AGE	0-6 months	6-12 months	1-2 years	2-3 years
To fit chest				
	41	46	51	56 cm
	16	18	20	22 in
Actual chest measurement				
	47	53	57	63 cm
	18½	20¾	22½	24¾ in
Full length, from shoulder				
	24	28	32	38 cm
	9½	11	12½	15 in
Sleeve length				
	15	17	20	24 cm
	6	6½	8	9½ in

YARN
Jody Long Ciao
4 [4: 5: 6] x 50g balls in Chrome 004

NEEDLES
1 pair 3.25 mm (no 10) (US 3) needles
1 pair 4 mm (no 8) (US 6) needles

BUTTONS - 5 [5: 6: 6]

TENSION
20 sts and 40 rows to 10 cm (4 in) measured over eyelet patt using 4 mm (US 6) needles.

ABBREVIATIONS
See inside front flap

BACK
Using 3.25 mm (US 3) needles cast on 47 [53: 57: 63] sts.
Work in g st for 6 [6: 8: 8] rows, ending with RS facing for next row.
Change to 4 mm (US 6) needles.
Now work in eyelet patt as folls:
Row 1 (RS): K1, *yo, K2tog, rep from * to end.
Rows 2 to 10: Knit.
Row 11: K1, *yo, sl 1, K1, psso, rep from * to end.
Rows 12 to 20: Knit.
These 20 rows form patt.
Cont in patt until Back meas 14 [17: 20: 25] cm (5½ [6½: 8: 9¾] in), ending with RS facing for next row.

Shape Armholes
Keeping patt correct, cast off 2 sts at beg of next 2 rows.
43 [49: 53: 59] sts.
Dec 1 st at each end of next and 3 [3: 2: 3] foll alt rows, then on foll 1 [2: 3: 3] 4th rows. 33 [37: 41: 45] sts.
Cont straight until armhole meas 10 [11: 12: 13] cm (4 [4¼: 4¾: 5] in), ending with RS facing for next row.

Shape Shoulders
Keeping patt correct, cast off 4 [4: 5: 5] sts at beg of next 2 rows, then 4 [5: 5: 6] sts at beg of foll 2 rows.
Break yarn and leave rem 17 [19: 21: 23] sts on a holder (for Neckband).

LEFT FRONT
Using 3.25 mm (US 3) needles cast on 25 [29: 31: 35] sts.
Work in g st for 6 [6: 8: 8] rows, ending with RS facing for next row.
Change to 4 mm (US 6) needles.
Work in eyelet patt as given for Back repeating the 20 row patt rep throughout, cont in patt until Left Front matches Back to beg of armhole shaping, ending with RS facing for next row.

Shape Armhole

Keeping patt correct, cast off 2 sts at beg of next row. 23 [27: 29: 33] sts.

Work 1 row.

Dec 1 st at armhole edge of next and 3 [3: 2: 3] foll alt rows, then on foll 1 [2: 3: 3] 4th rows. 18 [21: 23: 26] sts.

Cont straight until 16 [18: 20: 22] rows less have been worked than on Back to beg of shoulder shaping, ending with RS facing for next row.

Shape Front Neck

Next row (RS): Patt 16 [18: 21: 23] sts and turn, leaving rem 2 [3: 2: 3] sts on a holder (for Neckband). 16 [18: 21: 23] sts.

Keeping patt correct, dec 1 st at neck edge of next 4 [4: 6: 6] rows, then on foll 4 [5: 5: 6] alt rows. 8 [9: 10: 11] sts.

Work 3 rows, ending with RS facing for next row.

Shape Shoulders

Keeping patt correct, cast off 4 [4: 5: 5] sts at beg of next row.

Work 1 row.

Cast off rem 4 [5: 5: 6] sts.

RIGHT FRONT

Using 3.25 mm (US 3) needles cast on 25 [29: 31: 35] sts.

Work in g st for 6 [6: 8: 8] rows, ending with RS facing for next row.

Change to 4 mm (US 6) needles.

Work in eyelet patt as given for Back repeating the 20 row patt rep throughout, cont in patt until Right Front matches Back to beg of armhole shaping, ending with RS facing for next row.

Shape Armhole

Work 1 row.

Keeping patt correct, cast off 2 sts at beg of next row. 23 [27: 29: 33] sts.

Dec 1 st at armhole edge of next and 3 [3: 2: 3] foll alt rows, then on foll 1 [2: 3: 3] 4th rows. 18 [21: 23: 26] sts.

Cont straight until 16 [18: 20: 22] rows less have been worked than on Back to beg of shoulder shaping, ending with RS facing for next row.

Shape Front Neck

Next row (RS): K2 [3: 2: 3] and slip these sts onto a holder (for Neckband), patt to end. 16 [18: 21: 23] sts.

Keeping patt correct, dec 1 st at neck edge of next 4 [4: 6: 6] rows, then on foll 4 [5: 5: 6] alt rows. 8 [9: 10: 11] sts.

Work 4 rows, ending with **WS** facing for next row.

Shape Shoulders

Keeping patt correct, cast off 4 [4: 5: 5] sts at beg of next row.

Work 1 row.

Cast off rem 4 [5: 5: 6] sts.

SLEEVES

Using 3.25 mm (US 3) needles cast on 25 [27: 29: 31] sts.

Work in g st for 6 [6: 8: 8] rows, ending with RS facing for next row.

Change to 4 mm (US 6) needles.

Work in eyelet patt as given for Back repeating the 20 row patt rep throughout **and at same time** shaping sides by inc 1 st at each end of next [3rd: 5th: 7th] and every foll 6th [6th: 6th: 8th] row

until there are 33 [37: 37: 51] sts, then on 3 [3: 5: -] foll 8th [8th: 8th: -] rows. 39 [43: 47: 51] sts.

Cont straight until Sleeve meas 15 [17: 20: 24] cm (6 [6¾: 8: 9½] in), ending with RS facing for next row.

Shape Top

Keeping patt correct, cast off 2 sts at beg of next 2 rows. 35 [39: 43: 47] sts.

Dec 1 st at each end of next 3 [5: 5: 7] rows, then on 3 foll 4th rows, then on foll 5 [5: 7: 7] alt rows, then on foll row, ending with RS facing for next row.

Cast off rem 11 sts.

MAKING UP

Join both shoulder seams.

Neckband

With RS facing, using 3.25 mm (US 3) needles, slip 2 [3: 2: 3] sts on right front holder onto right needle, rejoin yarn and pick up and knit 14 [15: 18: 19] sts up right side of front neck, K across 17 [19: 21: 23] sts on back holder, pick up and knit 14 [15: 18: 19] sts down left side of front neck, then K across 2 [3: 2: 3] sts on left front holder. 49 [55: 61: 67] sts.

Work in g st for 4 [4: 6: 6] rows, ending with **WS** facing for next row.

Cast off in **knitwise** (on **WS**).

Button Band

With RS facing, using 3.25 mm (US 3) needles, pick up and knit 53 [61: 71: 85] sts evenly down entire left front opening edge, from top of Neckband to cast-on edge.

Work in g st for 6 rows, ending with **WS** facing for next row.

Cast off in **knitwise** (on **WS**).

Buttonhole Band

With RS facing, using 3.25 mm (US 3) needles, pick up and knit 53 [61: 71: 85] sts evenly up entire right front opening edge, from cast-on edge to top of Neckband.

Work in g st for 3 rows, ending with RS facing for next row.

Row 4 (RS): K1 [1: 2: 1], *K2tog, yo (to make a buttonhole), K10 [12: 11: 14], rep from * 3 [3: 4: 4] times more, K2tog, yo (to make 5th [5th: 6th: 6th] buttonhole), K2.

Work in g st for a further 2 rows, ending with **WS** facing for next row.

Cast off in **knitwise** (on **WS**).

Join side seams. Join sleeve seams. Sew sleeves into armholes. Sew on buttons.

Pin out garment to measurements given and cover with damp cloths and leave to dry naturally. See ball band for washing and further care instructions.

SOFIA

SIZES

AGE	0-6 months	6-12 months	1-2 years	2-3 years
To fit chest				
	41	46	51	56 cm
	16	18	20	22 in
Actual chest measurement				
	45	51	56	62 cm
	17¾	20	22	24½ in
Full length, from back neck				
	21	25	29	35 cm
	8¼	9¾	11½	13¾ in
Sleeve length				
	15	17	20	24 cm
	6	6½	8	9½ in

YARN

Jody Long Ciao
3 [4: 4: 5] x 50g balls in Celadon 012

NEEDLES

1 pair 3.25 mm (no 10) (US 3) needles
1 pair 4 mm (no 8) (US 6) needles
Cable needle

BUTTONS - 3 [3: 3: 3]

TENSION

22 sts and 30 rows to 10 cm (4 in) measured over st st using 4 mm (US 6) needles.

ABBREVIATIONS

See inside front flap

SPECIAL ABBREVIATION

C12B = slip next 6 sts onto cable needle and leave at back of work, K6, then K6 from cable needle.

BACK

Using 3.25 mm (US 3) needles cast on 85 [93: 103: 111] sts.
Row 1 (RS): K1, *P1, K1, rep from * to end.
Row 2: P1, *K1, P1, rep from * to end.
These 2 rows form rib.
Work a further 3 [3: 5: 5] rows in rib, ending with **WS** facing for next row.
Next row (WS): P3 [4: 3: 4], P2tog, *P1, P2tog, rep from * to last 2 [3: 2: 3] sts, P2 [3: 2: 3]. 58 [64: 70: 76] sts.
Change to 4 mm (US 6) needles.
Beg with a K row, work in st st as folls:
Dec 1 st at each end of next [3rd: 3rd: 7th] row, then on 1 [2: 2: 2] foll 4th [6th: 8th: 10th] rows, then on 2 [1: 1: 1] foll 6th [8th: 10th: 12th] rows. 50 [56: 62: 68] sts.
Work 5 [7: 9: 13] rows, ending with RS facing for next row.

Shape Raglan Armholes

Cast off 3 sts at beg of next 2 rows. 44 [50: 56: 62] sts.

0-6 Months and 6-12 Months Only

Dec 1 st at each end of next row. 42 [48] sts.
Work 3 rows, ending with RS facing for next row.

1-2 Years and 2-3 Years Only

Dec 1 st at each end of next [2: 4] rows. [52: 54] sts.

6-12 Months, 1-2 Years and 2-3 Years Only

Dec 1 st at each end of next and [1: 2: 3] foll alt rows. [44: 46: 46] sts.

Work 1 row, ending with RS facing for next row.

All Sizes

Cast off rem 42 [44: 46: 46] sts.

LEFT FRONT

Using 3.25 mm (US 3) needles cast on 40 [44: 48: 52] sts.

Row 1 (RS): *K1, P1, rep from * to last 2 sts, K2.

Row 2: *K1, P1, rep from * to end.

These 2 rows form rib.

Work a further 3 [3: 5: 5] rows in rib, ending with **WS** facing for next row.

Next row (WS): P1 [1: 2: 2], (P2tog, P1) 13 [7: 15: 8] times, P0 [1: 1: 1], (P2tog, P1) 0 [7: 0: 8] times, P0 [0: 0: 1]. 27 [30: 33: 36] sts.

Change to 4 mm (US 6) needles.

Beg with a K row, work in st st as folls:

Dec 1 st at beg of next [3rd: 3rd: 7th] row, then on 1 [2: 2: 2] foll 4th [6th: 8th: 10th] rows, then on 2 [1: 1: 1] foll 6th [8th: 10th: 12th] rows. 23 [26: 29: 32] sts.

Work 2 [7: 9: 13] rows.

0-6 Months Only

Shape Front Neck

Next row (WS): Cast off 11 sts **purlwise**, P to end. 12 sts.

Dec 1 st at neck edge of next 2 rows. 10 sts.

All Sizes

Shape Raglan Armholes

Cast off 3 sts, K to last 2 [0: 0: 0] sts, (K2tog) 1 [0: 0: 0] times. 6 [23: 26: 29] sts.

0-6 Months Only

Next row (WS): P2tog, P to end. 5 sts.

6-12 Months Only

Next row (WS): Cast off 12 sts **purlwise**, P to end. [11] sts.

1-2 Years and 2-3 Years Only

Next row (WS): Purl.

Next row: K2tog, K to end. [25: 28] sts.

Shape Front Neck

Next row (WS): Cast off [15: 11] sts **purlwise**, P to last 2 sts, P2tog. [9: 16] sts.

6-12 Months and 1-2 Years Only

Next row (RS): K2tog, K to last 2 sts, K2tog. [9: 7] sts.

Dec 1 st at neck edge of next and 2 [0] foll rows. [6: 6] sts.

2-3 Years Only

Dec 1 st at each end of next 2 rows. [12] sts.

Next row (RS): K2tog, K to last 2 sts, K2tog.

Next row: P2tog, P to end.

Rep last 2 rows once more. [6] sts.

All Sizes

Work 3 rows dec 1 st at raglan edge in 1st and foll 0 [2nd: 2nd: 2nd] row **and at same time** dec 1 st at neck edge in 1st and foll alt row. 2 sts.

Next row (RS): P2tog. Fasten off.

RIGHT FRONT

Using 3.25 mm (US 3) needles cast on 40 [44: 48: 52] sts.

Row 1 (RS): K2, *P1, K1, rep from * to end.

Row 2: *P1, K1, rep from * to end.

These 2 rows form rib.

Work a further 3 [3: 5: 5] rows in rib, ending with **WS** facing for next row.

Next row (WS): P1 [1: 2: 2], (P2tog, P1) 13 [7: 15: 8] times, P0 [1: 1: 1], (P2tog, P1) 0 [7: 0: 8] times, P0 [0: 0: 1]. 27 [30: 33: 36] sts.

Change to 4 mm (US 6) needles.

Beg with a K row, work in st st as folls:

Dec 1 st at end of next [3rd: 3rd: 7th] row, then on 1 [2: 2: 2] foll 4th [6th: 8th: 10th] rows, then on 2 [1: 1: 1] foll 6th [8th: 10th: 12th] rows. 23 [26: 29: 32] sts.

Work 1 [7: 10: 14] rows.

0-6 Months and 6-12 Months Only

Shape Front Neck

Next row (RS): Cast off 11 [12] sts, K to end. 12 [14] sts.

0-6 Months Only

Next row (WS): Purl.

Dec 1 st at neck edge of next 3 rows. 9 sts.

All Sizes

Shape Raglan Armholes

Cast off 3 sts, P to last 2 [0: 0: 0] sts, (P2tog) 1 [0: 0: 0] times. 5 [11: 26: 29] sts.

1-2 Years and 2-3 Years Only

Shape Front Neck

Next row (RS): Cast off [15: 11], K to last 2 sts, K2tog. [10: 17] sts.

Next row: P2tog, P to end. [9: 16] sts.

6-12 Months and 1-2 Years Only

Work [4: 2] rows dec 1 st at neck edge in every row **and at same time** dec 1 st at raglan edge in 1st row. [6: 6] sts.

2-3 Years Only

Dec 1 st at each end of next 2 rows. [12] sts.

Dec 1 st at neck edge of next 4 rows **and at same time** dec 1 st at raglan edge on next and foll alt row. [6] sts.

All Sizes

Work 3 rows dec 1 st at neck edge in 1st and foll alt row **and at same time** dec 1 st at raglan edge in 1st and foll 0 [2nd: 2nd: 2nd] row. 2 sts.

Next row (WS): P2tog. Fasten off.

SLEEVES

Using 3.25 mm (US 3) needles cast on 51 [51: 55: 57] sts.

Work 5 [5: 7: 7] rows in rib as given for Back, ending with **WS** facing for next row.

Next row (WS): P2 [2: 1: 2], P2tog, *P1, P2tog, rep from * to last 2 [2: 1: 2] sts, P2 [2: 1: 2]. 35 [35: 37: 39] sts.

Change to 4 mm (US 6) needles.

Beg with a K row, work in st st as folls:

Inc 1 st at each end of 13th [9th: 7th: 7th] and every foll 16th [8th: 6th: 6th] row to 39 [43: 45: 45] sts, then on every foll - [-: 8th: 8th] row until there are - [-: 49: 53] sts.

Cont straight until Sleeve meas 15 [17: 20: 24] cm (6 [6¾: 8: 9½] in), ending with RS facing for next row.

Shape Raglans

Cast off 3 sts at beg of next 2 rows. 33 [37: 43: 47] sts.

0-6 Months and 6-12 Months Only

Dec 1 st at each end. 31 [35] sts.

Work 3 rows, ending with RS facing for next row.

1-2 Years and 2-3 Years Only

Dec 1 st at each end of next 2 rows. [39: 43] sts.

6-12 Months, 1-2 Years and 2-3 Years Only

Dec 1 st at each end of next and [1: 2: 4] foll alt rows. [31: 33: 33] sts.

Work 1 row, ending with RS facing for next row.

All Sizes

Cast off rem 31 [31: 33: 33] sts.

YOKE

Join raglan seams.

Using 4 mm (US 6) needles cast on 18 sts **loosely**.

Next row (WS): K1, P2, K3, (inc **purlwise** into next st) 6 times, K3, P2, K1. 24 sts.

Now work in patt as folls:

Row 1 (RS): K3, P3, K12, P3, K3.

Row 2: K1, P2, K3, P12, K1, wrap next st (by slipping next st from left needle onto right needle, taking yarn to opposite side of work between needles and then slipping same st back onto left needle - when working back across wrapped sts work the wrapped st and the wrapping loop tog as one st) and turn.

Row 3: P1, K12, P3, K3.

Row 4: K1, P2, K1, wrap next st and turn.

Row 5: P1, K3.

Row 6: K1, P2, K3, P12, K3, P2, K1.

Row 7: K3, P3, C12B, P3, K3.

Row 8: K1, P2, K3, P12, K1, wrap next st and turn.

Row 9: P1, K12, P3, K3.

Row 10: K1, P2, K1, wrap next st and turn.

Row 11: P1, K3.

Row 12: K1, P2, K3, P12, K3, P2, K1.

Row 13: K3, P3, K12, P3, K3.

Row 14: K1, P2, K3, P12, K1, wrap next st and turn.

Row 15: P1, K12, P3, K3.

Row 16: K1, P2, K1, wrap next st and turn.

Row 17: P1, K3.

Row 18: K1, P2, K3, P12, K3, P2, K1.

These 18 rows for patt.

Cont in patt until long edge of Yoke is approx 60 [62: 66: 66] cm (23¾ [24½: 26: 26] in), and of sufficient length to fit around top of cardigan, finishing with after Row 11 of patt and **WS** facing for next row.

Next row (WS): K1, P2, K3, (P2tog) 6 times, K3, P2, K1. 18 sts.

Cast off in patt **loosely**.

MAKING UP

Neckband

Sew yoke (longer edge) evenly around top of cardigan.

With RS facing, using 3.25 mm (US 3) needles pick up and knit 77 [79: 89: 95] sts evenly along top edge of Yoke.

Row 1 (WS): K1, *P1, K1, rep from * to end.

Row 2: K1, *K1, P1, rep from * to last 2 sts, K2.

These 2 rows form rib.

Work a further 2 [2: 4: 4] rows in rib, ending with **WS** facing for next row.

Cast of in rib (on **WS**).

Button Band

With RS facing and using 3.25 mm (US 3) needles, pick up and knit sts evenly down entire left front opening edge as folls; Pick up and knit 4 [4: 6: 6] sts along neckband, 21 sts down yoke edge, 20 [32: 42: 54] sts down front opening edge, then pick up and knit 6 [6: 8: 8] sts along rib to cast-on edge. 51 [63: 77: 89] sts.

Beg with row 1, work in rib as given for Neckband for 6 rows, ending with **WS** facing for next row.

Cast off in rib (on **WS**).

Buttonhole Band

With RS facing and using 3.25 mm (US 3) needles, pick up and knit sts evenly up entire right front opening edge as folls; Pick up and knit 6 [6: 8: 8] sts along rib from cast-on edge, 20 [32: 42: 54] sts up front opening edge, 21 sts up yoke edge, then pick up and knit 4 [4: 6: 6] sts along neckband. 51 [63: 77: 89] sts.

Beg with row 1, work in rib as given for Neckband for 2 rows, ending with **WS** facing for next row.

Row 3 (WS): Rib 2, *P2tog, yo (to make a buttonhole), rib 8 [8: 10: 10], rep from * once more, P2tog, yo (to make 3rd buttonhole), rib to end.

Work 3 more rows in rib, ending with **WS** facing for next row.

Cast off in rib (on **WS**).

Join side and sleeve seams. Sew on buttons.

Pin out garment to measurements given, cover with damp cloths and leave to dry naturally. See ball band for washing and further care instructions.

SKILL LEVEL

VENICE

SIZES

AGE	0-6 months	6-12 months	1-2 years	2-3 years
To fit chest				
	41	46	51	56 cm
	16	18	20	22 in
Actual chest measurement				
	45	51	56	62 cm
	17¾	20	22	24¼ in
Full length, from back neck				
	24	28	32	38 cm
	9½	11	12½	15 in
Sleeve length				
	15	17	20	24 cm
	6	6½	8	9½ in

YARN

Jody Long Ciao
A 2 [3: 3: 4] x 50g balls in Chrome 004
B 2 [2: 2: 3] x 50g balls in Alabaster 002

NEEDLES

1 pair 3.25 mm (no 10) (US 3) needles
1 pair 4 mm (no 8) (US 6) needles

BUTTONS - 5 [5: 5: 6]

TENSION

22 sts and 30 rows to 10 cm (4 in) measured over striped st st using 4 mm (US 6) needles.

ABBREVIATIONS

See inside front flap

BACK

Using 3.25 mm (US 3) needles and yarn **A** cast on 58 [66: 70: 78] sts.

Row 1 (RS): *K2, P2, rep from * to last 2 sts, K2.
Row 2: *P2, K2, rep from * to last 2 sts, P2.
These 2 rows form rib.
Cont in rib for a further 7 [7: 9: 9] rows, ending with **WS** facing for next row.
Next row (WS): P4 [5: 6: 2], P2tog, (P5 [4: 6: 6], P2tog), 7 [9: 7: 9] times, P3 [5: 6: 2]. 50 [56: 62: 68] sts.
Change to 4 mm (US 6) needles.
Beg with a K row, now work in striped st st as folls:
Using yarn **B**, work 4 rows.
Using yarn **A**, work 4 rows.
These 8 rows form striped st st.
Cont in striped st st until Back meas 12 [15: 18: 23] cm (4¾ [6: 7: 9] in), ending with RS facing for next row.

Shape Raglan Armholes

Keeping stripes correct, cast off 3 [3: 3: 4] sts at beg of next 2 rows. 44 [50: 56: 60] sts.

1-2 and 2-3 Years Only

Next row (RS): K1, sl 1, K1, psso, K to last 3 sts, K2tog, K1.
Next row: P1, P2tog, P to last 2 sts, P2tog tbl, P1.
Rep the last 2 rows [0: 1] time more. [52: 52] sts.

For All Sizes

Next row (RS): K1, sl 1, K1, psso, K to last 3 sts, K2tog, K1.
Next row: Purl.
These 2 rows set raglan armhole shaping.
Dec 1 st at each end as before on next and foll 11 [13: 13: 13] alt rows. 18 [20: 22: 22] sts.
Work 1 row, ending with RS facing for next row.
Break yarn and leave rem 18 [20: 22: 22] sts on a holder (for Hood).

LEFT FRONT

Using 3.25 mm (US 3) needles and yarn **A** cast on 27 [31: 35: 35] sts.

Row 1 (RS): *K2, P2, rep from * to last 3 sts, K3.

Row 2: K1, P2, *K2, P2 rep from * to end.

These 2 rows form rib.

Cont in rib for a further 7 [7: 9: 9] rows, ending with **WS** facing for next row.

Next row (WS): P4 [2: 1: 4], P2tog, (P4 [3: 3: 6], P2tog) 3 [5: 6: 3] times, P3 [2: 2: 5]. 23 [25: 28: 31] sts.

Change to 4 mm (US 6) needles.

Beg with a K row, work in striped st st as given for Back as folls:

Cont straight until Left Front matches Back to beg of raglan armhole shaping, ending with RS facing for next row and ending on the same stripe as Back to start of raglan shaping.

Shape Raglan Armhole

Keeping stripes correct, cast off 3 [3: 3: 4] sts at beg of next row. 20 [22: 25: 27] sts.

Work 1 row, ending with RS facing for next row.

1-2 and 2-3 Years Only

Next row (RS): K1, sl 1, K1, psso, K to end.

Next row: P to last 3 sts, P2tog tbl, P1.

Rep the last 2 rows [0: 1] time more. [23: 23] sts.

For All Sizes

Next row (RS): K1, sl 1, K1, psso, K to end.

Next row: Purl.

These 2 rows set raglan armhole shaping.

Dec 1 st at raglan edge as before on next and foll 10 [12: 12: 11] alt rows, and ending with **WS** facing for next row. 8 [8: 9: 10] sts.

Shape Front Neck

Keeping patt correct, cast off 4 [4: 5: 4] sts at beg of next row. 4 [4: 4: 6] sts.

0-6 Months, 6-12 Months and 1-2 Years Only

Next row (RS): K1, sl 1, K2tog, psso. 2 [2: 2] sts.

2-3 Years Only

Next row (RS): K1, sl 1, K1, psso, K1, K2tog. 4 sts.

Next row: P2tog, P2. 3 sts.

Next row: K1, sl 1, K1, psso. 2 sts.

For All Sizes

Next row (WS): P2tog. Fasten off.

RIGHT FRONT

Using 3.25 mm (US 3) needles and yarn **A** cast on 27 [31: 35: 35] sts.

Row 1 (RS): K1, *K2, P2, rep from * to last 2 sts, K2.

Row 2: *P2, K2, rep from * to last 3 sts, P2, K1.

These 2 rows form rib.

Cont in rib for a further 7 [7: 9: 9] rows, ending with **WS** facing for next row.

Next row (WS): P3 [2: 2: 5], P2tog, (P4 [3: 3: 6], P2tog) 3 [5: 6: 3] times, P4 [2: 1: 4]. 23 [25: 28: 31] sts.

Change to 4 mm (US 6) needles.

Beg with a K row, work in striped st st as given for Back as folls:

Cont straight until Right Front matches Back to beg of raglan armhole shaping, ending with **WS** facing for next row and ending on the same stripe as Back to start of raglan shaping.

Shape Raglan Armhole

Keeping stripes correct, cast off 3 [3: 3: 4] sts at beg of next row. 20 [22: 25: 27] sts.

1-2 and 2-3 Years Only

Next row (RS): K to last 3 sts, K2tog, K1.

Next row: P1, P2tog, P to end.

Rep the last 2 rows [0: 1] time more. [23: 23] sts.

For All Sizes

Next row (RS): K to last 3 sts, K2tog, K1.

Next row: Purl.

These 2 rows set raglan armhole shaping.

Dec 1 st at raglan edge as before on next and foll 9 [11: 11: 10] alt rows. 9 [9: 10: 11] sts.

Work 1 row, ending with RS facing for next row.

Shape Front Neck

Keeping patt correct work as folls:

Next row (RS): Cast off 4 [4: 5: 4] sts, K to last 3 sts, K2tog, K1. 4 [4: 4: 6] sts.

Work 1 row, ending with RS facing for next row.

0-6 Months, 6-12 Months and 1-2 Years Only

Next row (RS): Sl 1, K2tog, psso, K1. 2 [2: 2] sts.

2-3 Years Only

Next row (RS): (K2tog, K1) twice. 4 sts.

Next row: P2, P2tog. 3 sts.

Next row: K2tog, K1. 2 sts.

For All Sizes

Next row (WS): P2tog. Fasten off.

SLEEVES

Using 3.25 mm (US 3) needles and yarn **A** cast on 42 [42: 46: 46] sts.

Work in rib as given for Back for 9 [9: 11: 11] rows, ending with **WS** facing for next row.

Next row (WS): P3 [3: 1: 2], P2tog, (P5 [5: 4: 6], P2tog) 5 [5: 7: 5] times, P2 [2: 1: 2]. 36 [36: 38: 40] sts.

Change to 4 mm (US 6) needles.

Beg with a K row, work in striped st st as given for Back as folls:

Work 12 [4: 4: 4] rows, ending with RS facing for next row.

Next row (RS): K2, M1, K to last 2 sts, M1, K2. 38 [38: 40: 42] sts.

Keeping stripes correct and working all increases as set by last row, inc 1 st at each end of every foll 12th [8th: 8th: 8th] row to 40 [44: 48: 48] sts, then on every foll - [-: -: 10th] row until there are - [-: -: 52] sts.

Cont straight until Sleeve meas approx 15 [17: 20: 24] cm (6 [6½: 8: 9½] in), ending with RS facing for next row and ending on the same stripe as Back to start of raglan shaping.

Shape Raglan

Keeping stripes correct, cast off 3 [3: 3: 4] sts at beg of next 2 rows. 34 [38: 42: 44] sts.

Working all decreases as set by back raglan, dec 1 st at each end of next and foll 4th row, then on foll 9 [11: 12: 13] alt rows. 12 [12: 14: 14] sts.

Work 1 row, ending with RS facing for next row.

Cast off.

MAKING UP

Join raglan seams.

Hood

Using 4 mm (US 6) needles and yarn **A** cast on 23 [23: 23: 26] sts, with RS facing using the same needle and yarn work across the 18 [20: 22: 22] sts from back neck holder as folls: K3 [4: 4: 4], M1, (K4 [4: 3: 3], M1) 3 [3: 5: 5] times, K3 [4: 3: 3], cast on 23 [23: 23: 26] sts. 68 [70: 74: 80] sts.

Beg with a P row, work 3 rows in st st, ending with RS facing for next row.

Beg with a K row, work in striped st st as folls:

Using yarn **B**, work 4 rows.

Using yarn **A**, work 4 rows.

These 8 rows form striped st st.

Cont in striped st st until Hood meas 15 [17: 18: 19] cm (6 [6½: 7: 7½] in), ending with RS facing for next row.

Shape Top

Keeping stripes correct, cast off 23 [23: 25: 27] sts, at the beg of next 2 rows. 22 [24: 24: 26] sts.

Cont in patt until work meas 10 [10: 11: 12] cm (4 [4: 4¼: 4¾] in) **from cast-off sts,** ending with RS facing for next row.

Cast off.

Join side edges at top of hood to 23 [23: 25: 27] cast-off sts.

Hood Border

With RS facing, using 3.25 mm (US 3) needles and yarn **A** pick up and knit 39 [44: 46: 49] sts evenly along right side of hood, 22 [24: 24: 26] sts from top of hood and 39 [44: 46: 49] sts evenly along left side of hood. 100 [112: 116: 124] sts.

Row 1 (WS): K1, *P2, K2, rep from * to last 3 sts, P2, K1.

Row 2: K3, *P2, K2, rep from * to last st, K1.

These 2 rows form rib.

Work a further 5 [5: 7: 7] rows in rib, ending with RS facing for next row.

Cast off in rib.

Left Front Border

With RS facing using 3.25 mm (US 3) needles and yarn **A** pick up and knit 56 [68: 80: 88] sts evenly down left front opening edge, from start of neck shaping to cast-on edge.

Beg with row 1, work in rib as given for Hood Border for 4 rows, ending with **WS** facing for next row.

For a Girl

Work in rib for a further 5 rows, ending with RS facing for next row. Cast off in rib.

For a Boy

Row 5 (WS): Rib 3, *yo, work 2 tog (to make a buttonhole), rib 10 [13: 16: 14], rep from * 3 [3: 3: 4] times more, yo, work 2 tog (to make 5th [5th: 5th: 6th] buttonhole), rib 3.

Work in rib for a further 4 rows, ending with RS facing for next row. Cast off in rib.

Right Front Border

With RS facing using 3.25 mm (US 3) needles and yarn **A** pick up and knit 56 [68: 80: 88] sts evenly down right front opening edge, from cast-on edge to start of neck shaping.

Beg with row 1, work in rib as given for Hood Border for 4 rows, ending with **WS** facing for next row.

For a Girl

Row 5 (WS): Rib 3, *yo, work 2 tog (to make a buttonhole), rib 10 [13: 16: 14], rep from * 3 [3: 3: 4] times more, yo, work 2 tog (to make 5th [5th: 5th: 6th] buttonhole), rib 3.

Work a further 4 rows in rib, ending with RS facing or next row. Cast off in rib.

For a Boy

Work in rib for a further 5 rows, ending with RS facing for next row. Cast off in rib.

For Boy or Girl

Join side and sleeve seams. Placing row-ends of hood border halfway across front borders, sew hood evenly in position across sleeve tops and around neck edge. Sew on buttons.

Pin out garment to measurements given and cover with damp cloths and leave to dry naturally. See ball band for washing and further care instructions.

ZITA

SIZES
Completed blanket measures 86 cm (34 in) wide and 106 cm (41¾ in) long.

YARN
Jody Long Ciao
A 3 x 50g balls in Boysenberry 017
B 3 x 50g balls in Myrtle 010
C 3 x 50g balls in Avocado 011
D 3 x 50g balls in Marigold 015
E 3 x 50g balls in Dijon 016
F 3 x 50g balls in Fuchsia 019

NEEDLES
4 mm (no 8) (US 6) circular needle
4 mm (no 8) (US G-6) crochet hook

TENSION
28½ sts and 28½ rows to 10 cm (4 in) measured over patt using 4 mm (US 6) needles.

ABBREVIATIONS
See inside front flap

CROCHET ABBREVIATION
treble (double) crochet = yarn over and insert hook into the work, yarn over and draw through the work only, yarn over and draw through the first 2 loops only, yarn over and draw through the last two loops on the hook.

STRIPE SEQUENCE
Rows 1 and 2: Using yarn **A**.

Rows 3 to 10: Using yarn **B**.

Rows 11 and 12: Using yarn **A**.

Rows 13 to 20: Using yarn **C**.

Rows 21 and 22: Using yarn **A**.

Rows 23 to 30: Using yarn **D**.

Rows 31 and 32: Using yarn **A**.

Rows 33 to 40: Using yarn **E**.

Rows 41 and 42: Using yarn **A**.

Rows 43 to 50: Using yarn **F**.
These 50 rows form stripe sequence and are repeated throughout.

BLANKET
Using 4 mm (US 6) circular needle and yarn **A** cast on 244 sts.
Working back and forth in rows not rounds, work as folls:
Row 1 (RS): K2, *K9, K2tog, K8, inc knitwise into next st, rep from * to last 2 sts, K2.
Row 2: As row 1.
These 2 rows form patt and beg stripe sequence rows 1 and 2.
Now work as folls:
Beg with row **3** of stripe sequence, breaking off and joining in colours as required work in patt as now set and repeating the 50 row stripe sequence 6 times in total (ending with 8 rows in yarn **F**) and RS facing for next row.
Break off yarn **F** and join in yarn **A**.
Work 3 rows, ending with **WS** facing for next row.
Cast off knitwise (on **WS**).

MAKING UP
Weave in all ends securely.

Right Border
With RS facing, using a 4 mm (US G-6) crochet hook and yarn **A** work 1 treble (double) crochet into every other row along straight edge of blanket, starting from cast-on edge to cast-off edge, then fasten off.

Left Border
With RS facing, using a 4 mm (US G-6) crochet hook and yarn **A** work 1 treble (double) crochet into every other row along straight edge of blanket, starting from cast-off edge to cast-on edge, then fasten off.
Pin out to measurements given and cover with damp cloths and leave to dry naturally. See ball band for washing and further care instructions.